RESILIENCE

HOW WE HEAL

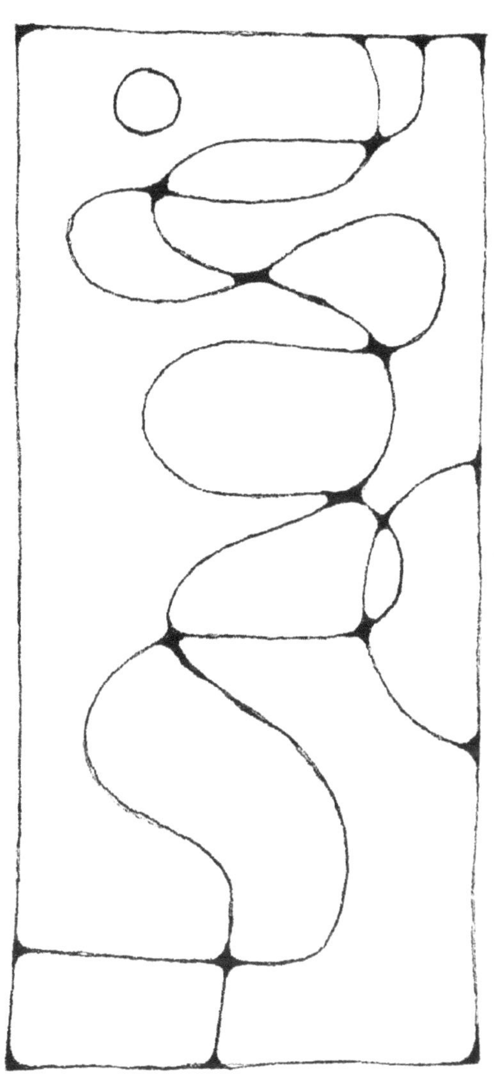

RESILIENCE

HOW WE HEAL

Curated by Becky Magnolia
Illustrated by Renee Simpson

Illustrations: Renee Simpson
www.reneesimpson.art
Cover Design: Becky Magnolia
Interior Layout Design: Becky Magnolia
Proofreading: Karin Nicely
www.serenpublishing.com

This book is dedicated
to the healing power
within us all

TABLE OF CONTENTS

renee s s

Hello, and welcome to our anthology!

To start this book, let's begin with a little backstory…

You know that sound a toaster makes when your toast is done? It's that perfect combination of a "pop" and a "bing." For me, toast always arrives with a little bit of excitement. "I'm here!" it says. "Ready for you to butter me up with your love!"

That "pop" is what I experienced in June 2023 while on a Zoom call with my artist friend Renee Simpson.

"Becky," she said, with her sweet Texan drawl, "I'm working on a new pen-and-ink series on the theme of resilience. Would you be willing to write something I could use with my art?"

Bing!

When Renee and I chat something vibrates between us. It's a spark of excitement and creativity. It's quite magical. Although Renee and I have never met in person—she is in Lubbock, while I'm here in Northeastern Florida—we still feel like long-lost sisters.

Without hesitation, as the metaphorical toast of inspiration popped up in my soul, I asked Renee if she'd be open to not just accepting writing from myself, but co-creating a book with me, pairing her illustrations with the words of people from all over the country. She loved the idea!

And so, here we are five months later, buttering up our idea with love. I now have a file folder full of raw, emotional, oh-so-beautiful submissions *and* a collection of Renee's twenty-two simple yet profound illustrations.

I have also teamed up with editor and friend Karin Nicely to select, curate, and ever so gently proofread these poems and stories. While you'll find some stories in this book are from renowned authors, publishers, storytellers, and songwriters, a number of the creators in this anthology are completely new to the trade. What an honor to get to work with such diverse writers!

I have divided the book into three categories: Heal, Raw, and Hope. Each grouping brings the reader in with a different kind of feeling.

Be sure to also check out the "About the Author" section at the end. It is a collection of bios written mostly by the authors. These little gems of writing with their unique styles and word choices each hold stories of their own of these fabulous writers' lives.

Throughout the book, I have included a handful of writings that are each titled as a "Facebook Post." These are friends' social media posts that struck a chord with me. Upon request, my friends generously allowed me to include them in the book.

As you read, I hope you are as inspired as I am by this honest and revealing collection of writing on the beauty and tenacity of the human experience.

And so, with a heart full of gratitude and wonder, I send thanks to Renee, Karin, the marvelous contributors to this book…and to *YOU,* the reader. May we all
find the strength to heal even from the deepest, darkest of
wounds.

In love and gratitude,

Becky Magnolia

HEAL

renee ss

Ally Pfeifer

Remember to Breathe

The dress was perfect. It was floor-length and black with elegant sparkles strewn across in swirl-like patterns. The heels were high, but I was only going to be standing in them for a matter of minutes. Sitting in the lobby, waiting for the time to line up outside the tall wooden doors is where I started to feel the rise of panic. I sat in that blue, plush chair and practiced diaphragmatic breathing: three-second inhale, three-second exhale. Such breathing slows the heart rate, and mine was currently going haywire. So I sat and breathed.

It was time to go into the stage room (a dark, little room on the wing of the stage). There was one girl in front of me. "At least I'm not first again," I thought. She went in, and I caught a glimpse of the crowd. I tried to clear my mind. I told myself that all I had to do was focus on what I was doing. I had to pretend I was alone in that auditorium so the sea of faces didn't overwhelm my anxiety and stage fright. The girl in front of me's performance felt like it took forever. When she was finished, we hugged. She wished me good luck. It was my turn. The doors opened.

The first thing that always hits you is the lights. They're so bright, as if you're walking into an expedition on the sun itself. Then I saw him. He was sitting in the most maniacal spot, positioned so that it was the first section of the audience the performer would see as they walked onto the stage. He wasn't supposed to be there; I didn't want him there. But I refused to let this cause me to falter in any way. I wasn't there for him anymore; I was there for me. I proceeded to the center of the stage. I lowered my head and breathed — in: one, two, three...out: one, two, three. "You can do this," I told myself. I lifted my chin and the music began.

The first song was a Mozart piece: joyful, upbeat, and Italian. I put on the face, attempted to portray the character. This was one I'd originally learned in my first semester. I nailed it. Song number two was a lullaby from the previous semester, and the first French piece I'd ever sung. The composer, Fauré, is known for his lengthy phrases. My breath-control was spot on. I lowered my head in preparation for the third and final piece.

I've known this song for years, but I had only just learned it in my lessons that semester — "Memory" by Andrew Lloyd Webber. This piece meant a lot to me. No longer was I to be a character, portraying a piece that I was assigned by my professor. I had a message for everyone there, and I was resolved to deliver it. I took a deep, determined breath and lifted my head to cue the accompanist to begin the introduction of the song.

It's not the easiest piece, with many tempo and key changes. The range in the piece branches more than two octaves. None of the semantics mattered though as the piano started to introduce my story. One measure before my entrance, deep inhale, and go...

Suddenly the crowd was there, hundreds of faces before me. I could see my professor, Dianna Campbell, sitting beside my middle school choir teacher (who had come just to see me perform) and Dr. Perinchief, a highly regarded, retired choral director at the college. I saw my grandmother and other relatives. I saw my mom, sitting alone in the second row. I saw my father, sitting in his manipulative seat with his wife and my little brother. All of my stage fright fell away as I looked them all in the eyes, into their hearts, and I told them what I'd been trying to say my entire life. I told them of the memories that I missed, as well as the ones that haunted me. I told them of the pain I'd been through in my eighteen battlesome years. I told them in that song about my one, single wish in life — to be happy again.

With tears stinging my eyes, I held the final note until there was no air left inside of me. The piano stopped ringing. The crowd roared in applause, coming to their feet. I bowed. I acknowledged my accompanist. I walked out of the lights and off of the stage. I felt exhilarated and free.

In that performance, I told them everything I needed to say, and I knew that they had finally heard me.

My name was on a cake, along with the rest of the music program graduates that performed that night. My name was spelled wrong (Ali instead of Ally), but I didn't care; my NAME was on a CAKE. After the small reception and many congratulations, I drove away with the biggest smile and the happiest tears streaming down my face. I felt the biggest relief in the history of relieving. From that moment on, I no longer felt the incessant need to make them understand. I no longer had to write letters and songs and poems. I no longer had to search for the perfect words. I had finally found the passageway. I found and sang the notes that gave them the understanding I had been working so hard to help them grasp. I was finally able to show them...me.

After that night, I no longer had to remember to breathe. After that night, breathing finally came naturally to me again.

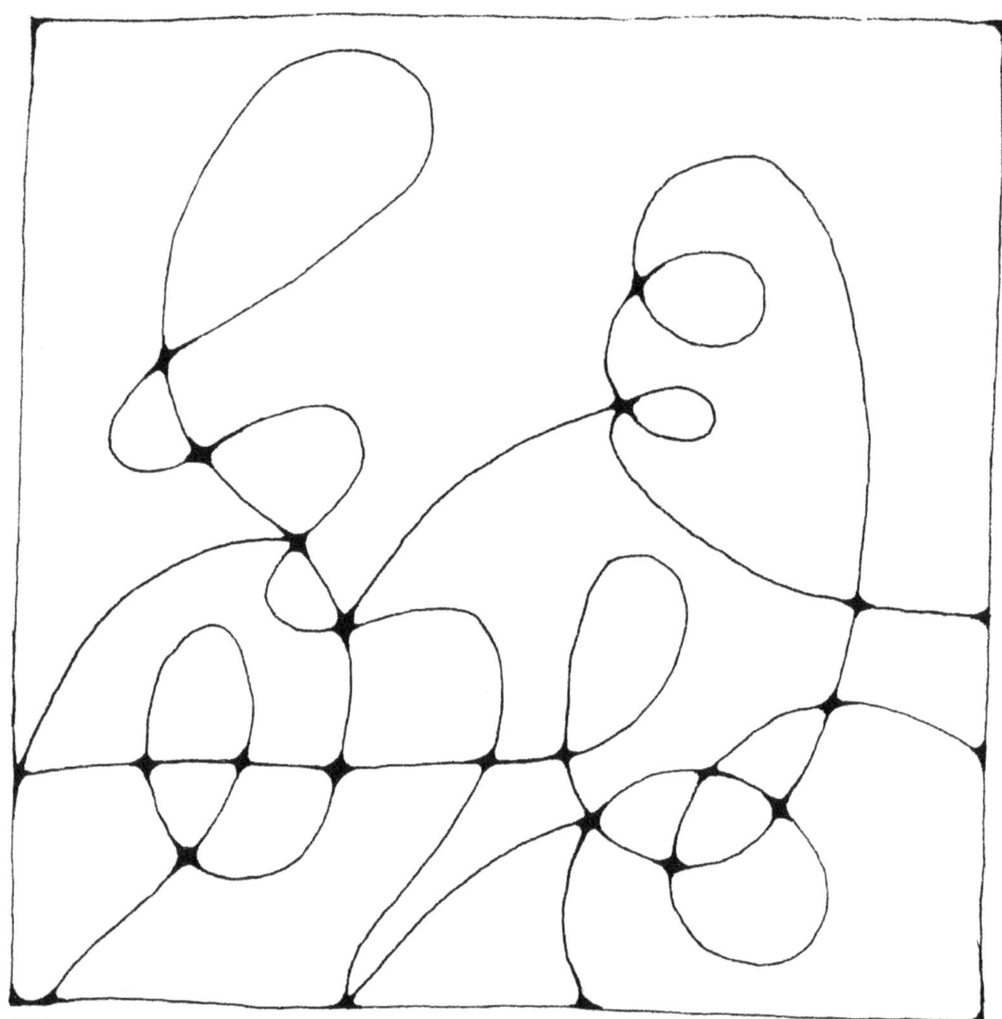

renee ss

Sugar Bear

Sometimes things happen for a reason, even if we don't know it at the time. The little things we do can have a deep and unexpected result.

Many years ago, I was a cop in Bushwick, Brooklyn. I worked with a lot of great cops. We all had nicknames. We didn't pick our own, of course. Instead, the rest of the guys would give you one. The name had to have some connection to you. It had to mean something. It didn't have to be anything great; it just had to say *you*.

Anyway, this is a little story of Larry. He was a big, heavy-set, friendly black man. He got the name Sugar Bear one day when we were all having lunch in the precinct and a commercial came on. It was for breakfast cereal that had an animated bear spokesman.

When the bear came on, one of the cops said, "Damn, Larry, you're on TV."

From that moment on, he was Sugar Bear. Sugar Bear worked in the precinct for many years. He even married one of the local girls. I never knew what her real name was — we all called her Goldie.

As we got older, one by one we retired, and as will often happen, many of us lost touch with each other. Sugar Bear moved down to South Carolina, and I moved first to Pennsylvania then to Florida.

After I retired, I accidently wrote a book. There is a story to that, but that is for another time. The book was a story of many of the things that happened in the precinct. Sometimes the stories were changed a bit, but all had some basis in fact. Now, in writing such a book, of course, all the names were changed. Although some of the nicknames remained because they added a touch of reality that wasn't very real. The book was never a big seller. I sold only five or six thousand copies.

As time went on, the internet came about. The guys from the precinct had started a Facebook page, and using it, many of us reconnected. One day, I saw Goldie online and asked her how Sugar Bear was doing. She told me the sad news that he had developed Alzheimer's and was in a nursing home. He no longer recognized her or the rest of his family. He no longer spoke or seemed to notice what was going on around him.

She told me she heard I wrote a book and asked how much it was. I just asked for her address and sent her a copy. It was no big deal; they are cheap enough. I forgot all about it.

A couple of months later, I received an email from Sugar Bear's daughter. She told me that she brought the book to the nursing and was reading it to him when he started to smile. He called her by name and told her he remembered some of the things in the book. She would go a couple of times a week, and he usually reacted like that.

A few years later, Sugar Bear passed on. His daughter wrote me to thank me for the book. She said that when she was reading the book, her father knew her and was happy. She thanked me for giving her father back to the family again. I almost cried that I had touched his family like that.

I guess the moral of this story is that a little thing you do may have a great effect on other people. Sometimes the little things you do are actually the biggest things in your life.

Hello, me.
The little me,
The one who didn't know who she was
But what she liked
And couldn't understand why everyone wouldn't just let her.
The one that liked cowboy boots and animal prints and wearing ALL THE ACCESSORIES AT ONCE
And didn't give a damn how well mixed or matched they were.
The one who loved to collect tiny stones and loved to play dress-up
But didn't see a need to be dressed up every Sunday to talk to an important man I'd never see
I mean the little tomboy that liked V necks and computers and video games and Indiana Jones
But would still defend the color pink with her dying breath because it's a beautiful color.
You with the thick brows before mental illness made you trim them
You with the ever-changing laugh and the Gameboy you carried everywhere
You who always had a new book under your arm when you weren't playing.
You who didn't care if your appearance was pristine walking out the door cuz you weren't here for everyone else's enjoyment and you don't need permission to exist
You with the loud voice and the fast mind before danger made you quiet
Hey, you!
YES YOU, I mean me.
Isn't it so sad that we haven't spoken in a while?
It's been so long since I last looked in and said
Are we happy?

It's been so long since I could ask that
Because it's been so long since the answer was yes.

A lifetime of finding out who closest to you I'd never trust
An eon of discovering just how many snake pits people can make of themselves
An eternity of proof that it was easier to just be quiet and fade out until it was all over.
An endless horizon of the landmines of the negative opinions and projections of those who dared utter the lie they loved you.
A mobius strip of certainty that I would never really be safe.
And so the only logical conclusion to build some walls that became a tower
That became a cage.
A cage of loneliness.
A trap of resentment.
A prison of self-hatred.
You never left that place unless concealed.
Concealed behind a mask of random assumed desirable traits and a desire to make everyone else happy.

Hello, me.
Yes me who grew into a tween and then teen still screaming behind that mask
The one who learned to only rock and stim in private
Because the kids thought it was weird
And the adults thought it was rude and might hurt you
But actually a child shouldn't /be/ in a chair all day
You just needed to move
And you need to move more when someone's yelling at you for something that's not your fault
The one who didn't know what dyscalculia was and just thought she was stupid cuz algebra HURT
The one who learned the hard way that relationships can be transactional
The one who tried really hard to meet everyone's expectations without getting the same manual as everyone else on what those were and why those were.
The one who found reprieve in putting it all down on paper.
The one who slowly lost her voice shortly after finding it

In favor of learning there was safety in hiding.
.
I'm sorry you felt you had to hide so much.
I'm happy that you were really bad at it. The parts no one could take away from you?
They're me now!
I'm sorry that you struggled so much.
And I'm sorry people went out of their way to make it harder.
Another diagnosis all these years later can't explain the cruelty you endured. You didn't
deserve it.
I'm sorry you felt like you had to take it out on you.
I'm sorry you lost the fight to keep your head above the water when it all came to it.
But I'm so proud of you for surviving.
For letting yourself forget the mask for a moment even if you kept it close by .
And I'm proud of you for eventually letting that mask crack apart.
For daring to see the sun in the narrow window.
For breaking down the damned wall and casting the broken fragments
Of the mask aside.
I am so proud of you.

Hello, me,
23, Nonbinary, Genderfluid, He/They/ sometimes She,
Finally taking hold of my voice again
Because it's mine and you gon hear me
When I have something to say
The loud me the proud me
The fight cuz I gotta me
The do what I oughta me
And the soft me and the simple me
Who loves chocolate,
And warm spicy foods and the smell of incense
And bad rage-inducing dad jokes,

And walking in the rain
And stomping in the puddles in giant boots
And a good story no matter how it's told,
Or what genre it fits
And applies the same principal to music
No matter how absolutely chaotic the playlist gets
The one who stims in public and doesn't apologize for needing to move
Because I'm still not here for anyone else's enjoyment
The one who learned it's okay to share yourself
The one who gives direct feedback because honesty is still your best policy
And who is still so full of love
That you bring it and inspire it everywhere you go
Hello me.
I love you. I see you. And I can't wait to see what we do.
Hello, me. It's so nice to finally meet you.

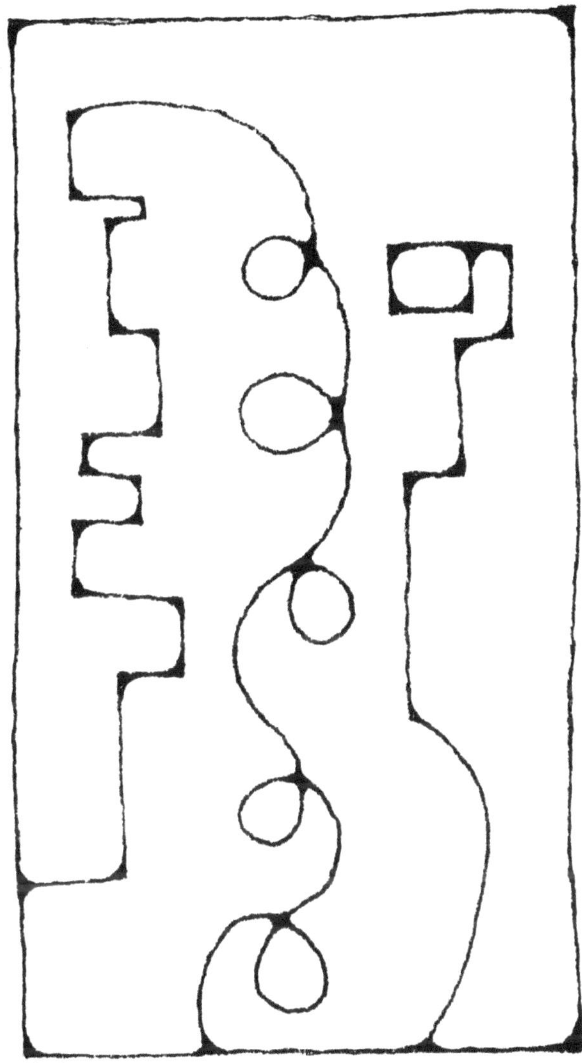

renee 55

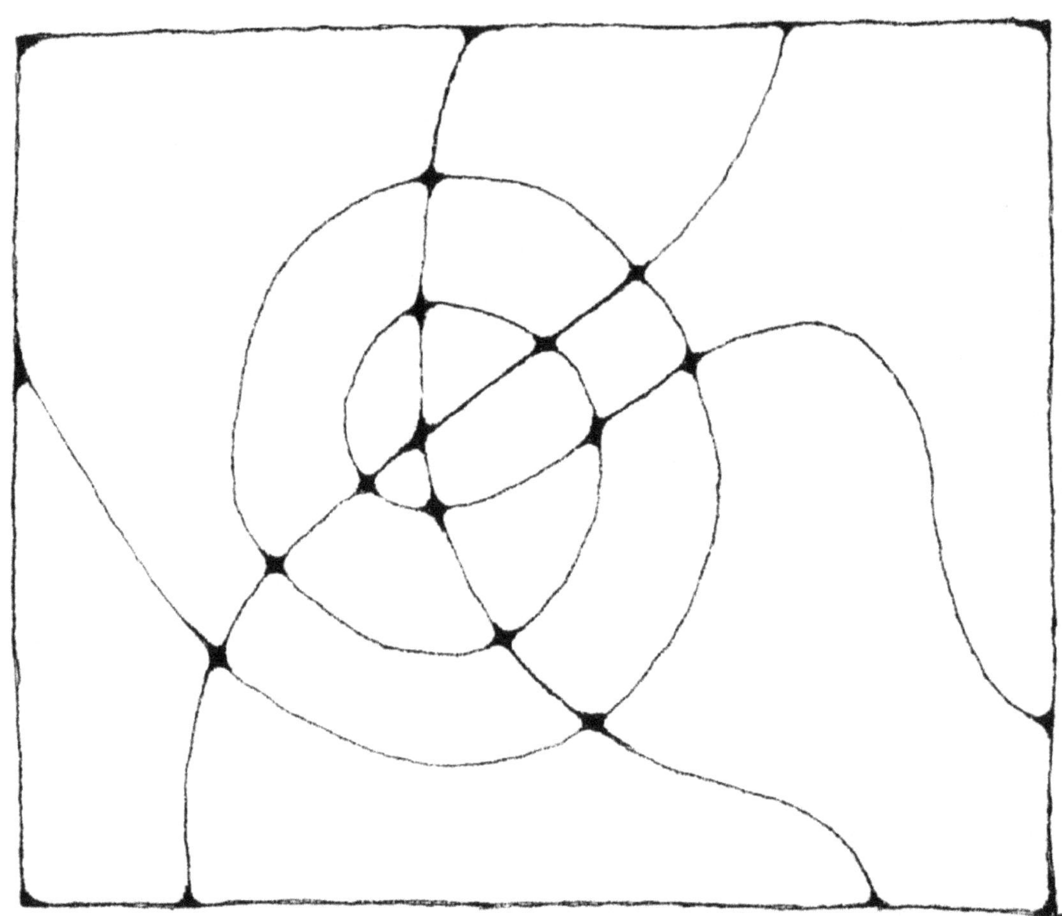

renee ss

Wonder Boy

1

"Strike three," the umpire called, and the boy hung his head and made his way back to the dugout.

"You suck, Carlos."

"Go play soccer or something."

"You strike out again, kid, I'm going to thump you."

And on and on. From fifteen voices. His teammates. Even the coach. "Sit down, Carlos. Jorge is going in for you."

Little league baseball in Puerto Rico was a serious thing. These twelve- and thirteen-year-olds had dreams of the big leagues. For some, it would be their only way off the island. And to do that, they had to win.

"Don't listen to those assholes," the old man said. They were riding on his bicycle after the game. Behind him, the old man could hear the boy crying.

"Maybe they are right, senor," he said between sniffles.

"Listen to me, boy," the old man said, his voice taking on that serious, deep tone when he wanted to convey something important to the boy. "Don't let anyone tell you what to do. You just need something…" and the old man paused before saying almost in a whisper, "special."

The old man and the boy entered the small store. The bell above the door tinkled. The boy sneezed twice. "I don't like this place, senor. It is old and…what is the word?"

"Dusty," the old man said. He resisted the urge to sneeze himself but was grateful for the cool air washing over his face.

"What is this place?"

"It's called a pawn shop," the old man said. He placed a protective hand on the boy's shoulder and guided him toward the back of the store.

"I can't believe my mother let you pick me up after the game," the boy complained and sneezed again. "When you said you had to talk to me, I thought you were going to impart some wisdom."

"Impart wisdom? You kill me, kid. Where did you learn that?"

The boy shrugged, his eyes taking in all the odd and exotic objects placed aimlessly on the counters. "Isn't that what old people do?"

"How many old people do you know?"

"Two. How many twelve-year-old kids do you know?"

"One too many," the old man said, and this time he did sneeze.

"You better have me home by four, or Mom is going to kill you," the boy said. He poked at some DVDs that were left on the counter.

"I know," the old man replied. "Don't touch those. Here it is."

Hanging on the wall amongst the grass blowers, golf clubs, and umbrellas was a baseball bat.

"Oh, wow," the boy cried. "Is that for me?"

The old man cradled the wooden bat in his hands and then presented it to the boy like a king bestowing a gift. "Of course it's for you. Do I play for the San Juan Pirates?"

The boy examined the 28" stick carefully. "What is this writing?" the boy asked.

On the side of the bat, etched by a burning chisel, were the words 'Wonder Boy.'

"There was a baseball movie called *The Natural* back in the '80s. The star of the team had a bat just like this. He was the best hitter on the team."

"This is for me?" the boy asked again, not believing his good fortune.

"It's a bit heavy for you now," the old man said. "But you'll grow into it."

The boy took a few swings with it. "But I am the worst hitter on the team."

"Maybe, but with a little practice, Wonder Boy will help you be as great as your hero, Roberto Clemente," the old man said. "You must be patient and practice hard."

The young boy stared up at the old man, a mischievous smile on his young face. "I knew you could do it, senor," he said.

The old man was confused. "Do what?"

"Impart wisdom. I am proud of you."

"Callate," the old man said, affectionately. "Let's get you home."

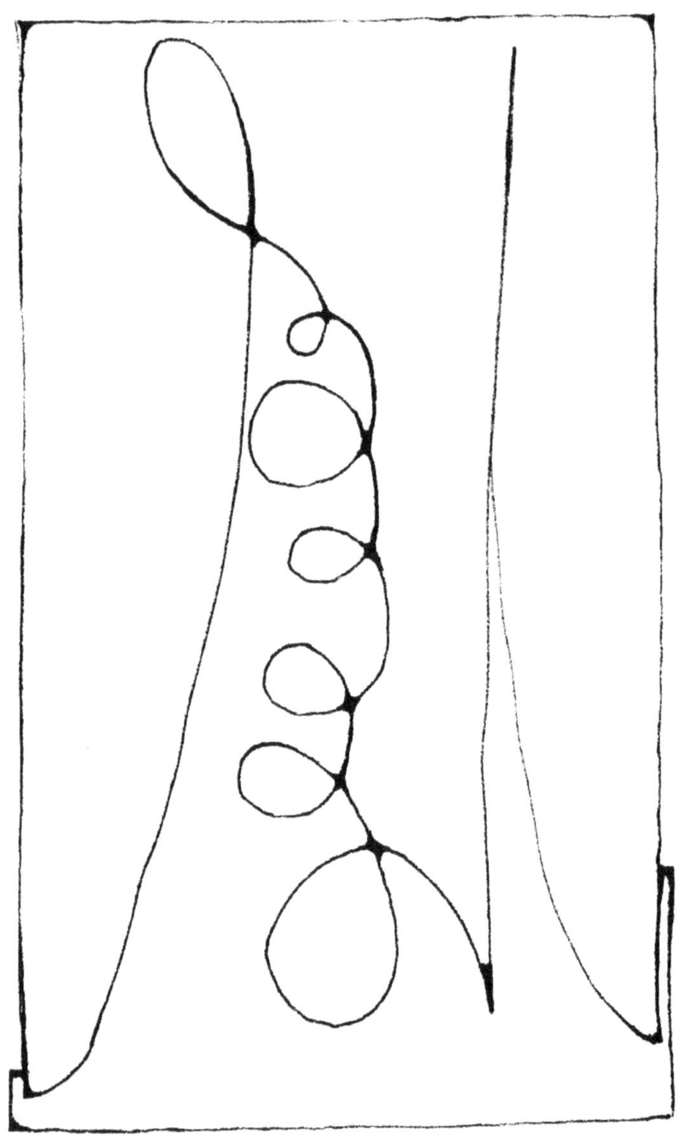

renee 55

Facebook Post, August 2023

Today is the 7th-year anniversary of the amputation of my right leg below the knee. I haven't given it much thought in recent years, but something is different this time.

A powerful thought came to me out of the blue, from nowhere, yesterday. It was: Oh my God, I only have one leg! That sucks! (lol).

I felt very sad and sorry for myself for all of about 2 minutes, then I got on with the wonderful life that I have, one that is far better than I ever imagined it would be.

I got through the initial shock of the surgery by telling myself that I would be back to 100% normal within a couple years. The person I have worked closely with who made my prosthetic leg is an amputee herself. To see her operate in the world, you would never know it. Complications with my surgery, setbacks, and stubborn weight gain have left me far from that goal today. I can walk about a hundred yards and then I have to rest for a long time before I can do it again.

I'm okay because I live in the present moment almost exclusively anymore. We read *Be Here Now* by Ram Dass in my family when I was in my late teens in 1970. In the past few years, I have started finally applying the spiritual tools in that amazing best-selling spiritual graphic novel and the results are in – pain and emotional upheaval are part of all human existence, but suffering is mostly optional.

Peace, love, and may the Force be with you.

May you never thirst.

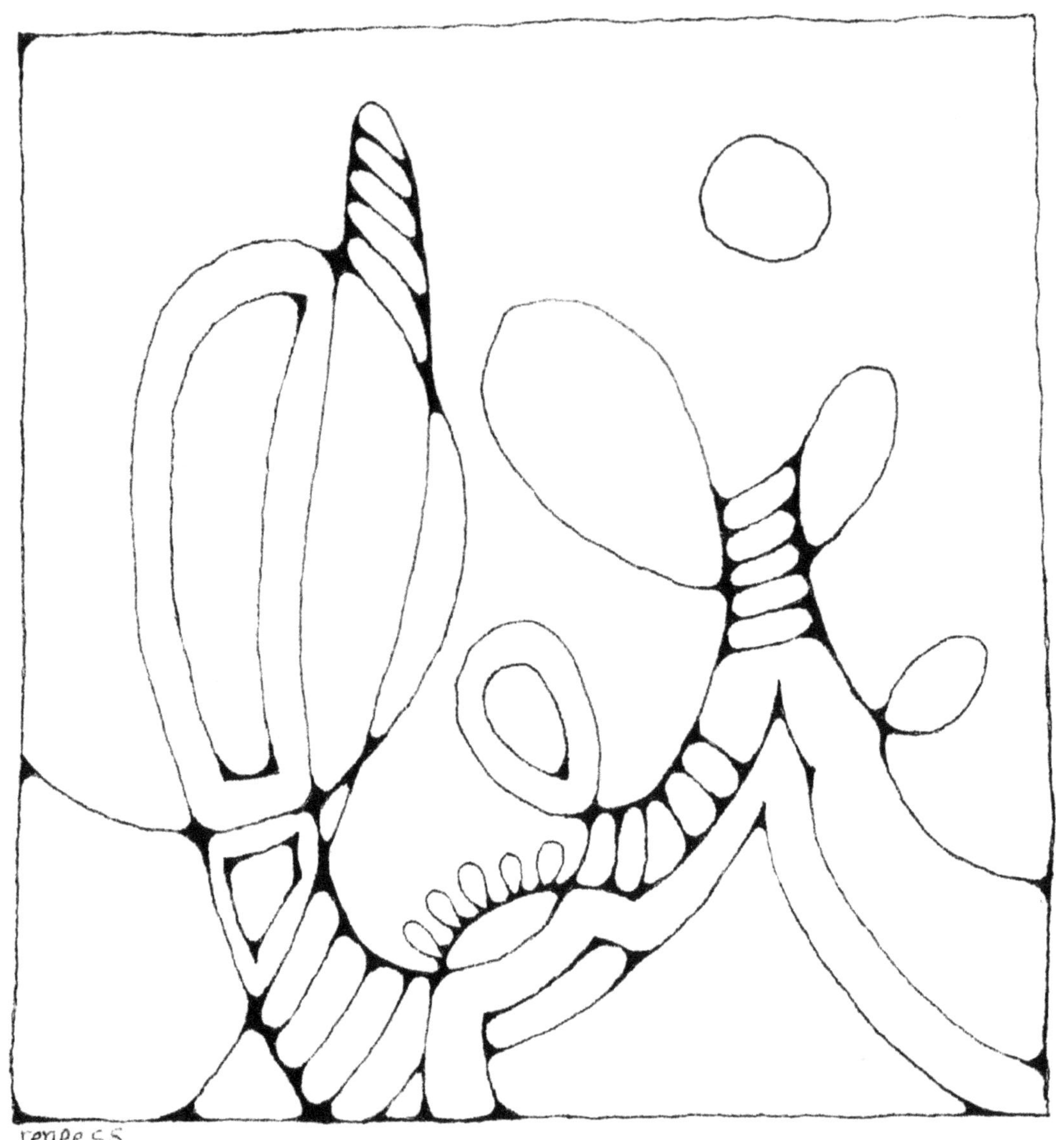

renee ss

Crystal Taylor

Red Tent Rebirth

The Shaman came in to help her be whole again

The Goddess arrived to be by her side

The drumming commenced, and the smoke filled the air

With Spirits surrounding her everywhere

All for a girl who was lost, but is found

Blackness and dark had filled her womb

And she encased her heart in a tomb

But the guides understood what needed to be done

The blackness was released and replaced with the sun

The Spirits escort her to the faerie place

And wipe the tears from her face

The goddesses await for her return

So to the red tent she goes now to learn

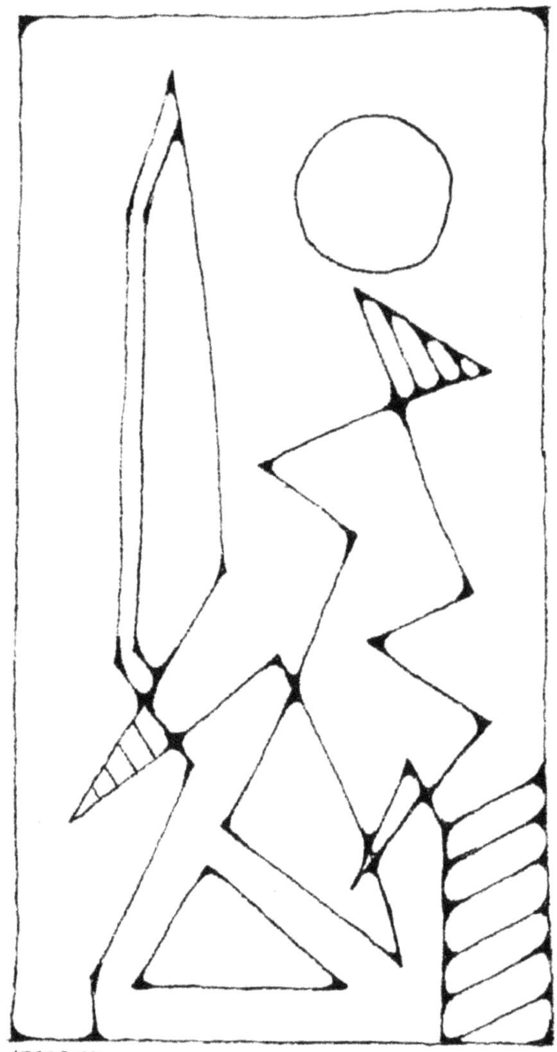

renee 55

S. J. Diamantos

Broken Moments

Crying eyes
Hidden scars
Agony inside
A wounded heart

Angry words
Hopeless dreams
This and more
Has shattered me

Cracking soul
Life upended
Stained glass window
Loving hands mended

Once sharp from grief
Now shaped anew
Beyond belief
A radiant view

Brightly shining
Luminescent delight
Broken moments defining
A beautiful sight

renee 55

The Journey

The other night, I met someone I knew from long ago,
She asked me if I recognized her pain-filled, tortured soul.
"Yes," I said, sick with dread, "I do," and then, I smiled.
"That soul was mine, once upon a time, when I was an ugly child.

"The beatings came, and cruelty reigned from six to twenty-nine.
A few good years to replenish the tears and again, the pain was mine.
I could not cope, with booze nor dope, nor life or death or time,
And so, my friend, I commenced to end the tortures in my mind."

She tried to grin, but the pain got in, and I watched her light go dark.
"How is it that you laugh and play with your children in the park?"
"My children brought me back to God, for without Him we are dead.
For the longest time, my days were hell, and I slowly lost my head…
But then one day, can't exactly say just how or who or why,
I couldn't go on with life so wrong and my soul began to fly.

"The freedom and serenity you see here in my eyes

Are solely due to Grace and Love and are part of one great prize…
Available by loving God and forgiving all that's wrong.
What comes of that is Hope and Peace and then in life you're strong."

The dream began to fade away; I reached to hold her close…
I woke to find my pillow wet – my throat all dry and choked.
I guess it's good to visit back to where healing all began,
To love and care and live again: The Journey of being Man.

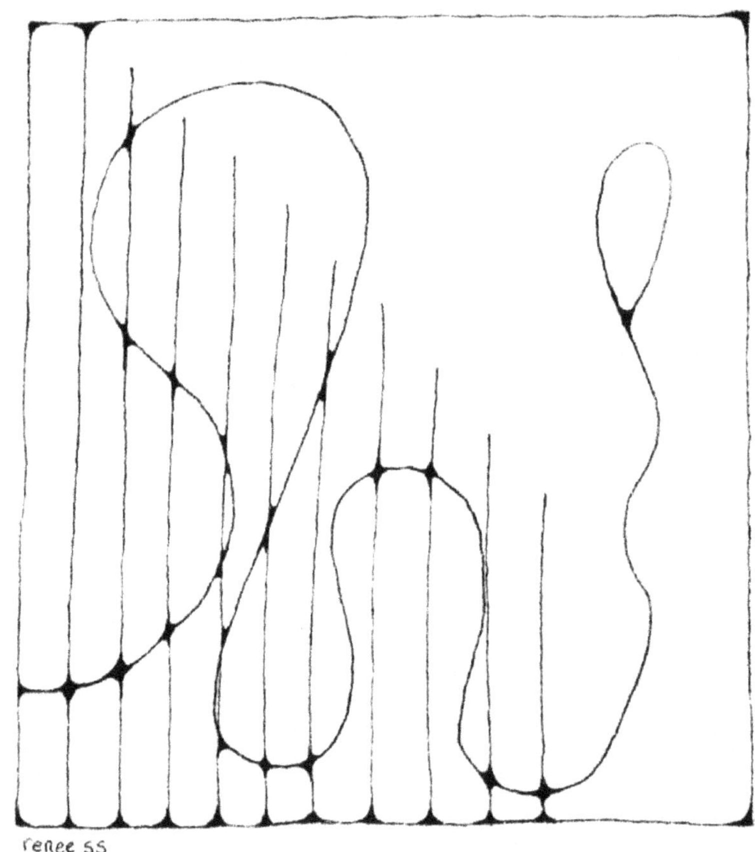

renee ss

Nikki Pennella

Alchemy of the Heart:
Fear's Transformation

What is this I hear?
Incessant chatter, doubt, and fear

A monster appears
Larger than life
Crippled in fear
How will I survive?

A tug of war
Inside my brain
Paralyzed and emotionally drained

Part of me desires for more
The other part shrinks, afraid to explore

What is it that I really fear?
My life is destined for my time here

If I am set up to win
Why my shine I choose to dim?

This jabberwocky isn't real
An illusion of the mind
Created to steal

A fire that burns within my heart
For my life is an important part

It's part of the fabric
Of all time
A golden thread
So divine

The jabberwocky,
Metaphor for fear
An opportunity to deeply heal

Put on a cloak of courage
With dignity I face
This larger-than-life illusion
I defeat it with my grace

As it vaporizes before me
Reduced to nothing but ash
I am left with only my SELF
And my earthly task

Now, I finally see the truth
I created this jabberwocky
Way back in my youth

In effort to protect
A deeply wounded me
I allowed it to distort my view and everything I see

I gave it so much power
It happily led me astray
Then it turned against me
I became its prey

Until the fateful day arrived…a battle to be won
The landscape dark and grey
Not one ray of sun

I'm reminded of my timeline and
The outcome of this day
I courageously picked up my sword
The jabberwocky slayed

In that moment, I realized
I was destined to win
I just needed to trust
My hero lies within

One tiny step of courage
Brought a monster to its knees
There is nothing that's impossible
For the one who chooses to BELIEVE!

Inspired by *Alice in Wonderland*

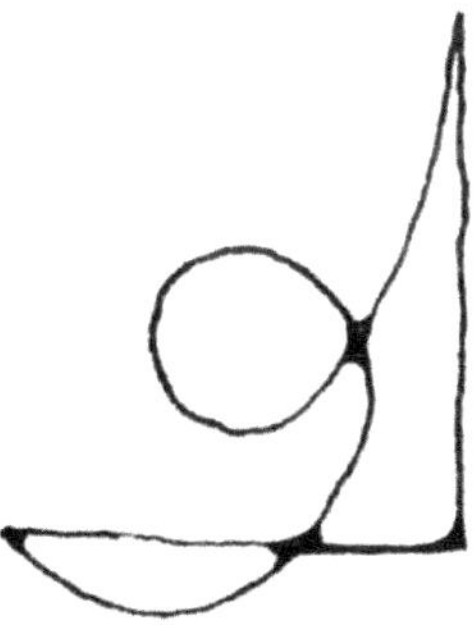

Mark's Musings

"This is my space. Venture closer and risk love, flight, or fight."

"Hand in hand, we trace emotional edges."

"Words can be sharp as a knife or soft as a cooing dove."

"How many times does your heart change in a lifetime?"

"Solitude allows the thirst for knowledge to bubble to the surface."

"Isolation is a state of mind. We can be alone in a crowd or find company in a field of flowers."

RAW

renee s s

The Waiting Room at the End of the World

It was an odd turn of events. I found myself seated in a dingy hospital room with a group of other admitted patients awaiting advanced imaging. The five months of chemo I'd received for Hodgkin's Lymphoma had eradicated the cancer but hadn't been kind to my body. I was underweight, bald, in a wheelchair, and on oxygen. I didn't know if the results of this test would give me hope that I'd be going home or leave the doctors further confused about how to help me.

As I looked up from my potent reverie, my eyes caught sight of a familiar face. An older man, he was probably at least sixty years older than my twenty-four. Pale and resigned to his fate, he was, like me, covered by the dull, worn fabric of a hospital gown — the great equalizer of human beings. He had been a professor of literature, a very good one, in fact, and I had been his student for Shakespeare I and II. I recalled the tattered shirt he had worn when walking into class one day, tearing at it with all the dramatics of a mad King Lear.

I'd approached him for help one afternoon. I'd sat in front of his desk with a "colorful" pile of papers. My ideas for the Romeo and Juliet assignment were scrawled onto scraps of paper and glued together on larger pages in an attempt to find some common thread between my disjointed musings. I found it impossible to organize my thoughts at that time, perhaps a side effect of the various drugs I had been experimenting with. He tried to help me find my voice as a writer. Later, when I decided to drop out of college, he gave me a WP (Withdraw Pass)[1] and wrote me a note saying that I was a bright young woman and that he sincerely hoped I would resume my education.

Now, here we were, the two of us together, in the waiting room at the end of the world. A young woman who had been running from her feelings and fears for years, fighting off self-destructive urges while clothed in the garments of a peace-loving hippie, now hanging on to the threads of a life she wished she had learned to love better. And an old man who, from all appearances, had lived a meaningful and respectable life, educating young adults and sharing his enthusiasm for great works of literature for decades. He and I were different in many ways, but in this room, we were simply human beings in hospital gowns, teetering precariously on the edge of the "now" and the "what's next?"

Should I say something? Should I thank him for encouraging me? Should I tell him I had returned to college and graduated with a bachelor's degree a few months before my cancer diagnosis? Did I have the physical strength or emotional energy to speak up from across the room to this man I thought I recognized? Was the fact that we had ended up very sick in this hospital room together depressing or a sign from God? While I pondered

---

[1] A Withdraw Pass grade is more merciful than a Withdraw Fail as it doesn't impose penalties on a student's GPA.

what to do, my name was called by the imaging technician, and before I knew it, I was whisked away to whatever destiny the Divine yet held for me.

Later, from the comfort and sanctuary of my home, I would read the obituary of my former professor. It was a pleasant story of a well-lived life. Fourteen years have passed since I saw him that day in the hospital. Every so often, I recall the surreal moment when our paths crossed one last time. I am not sure why God put us in that room together. Maybe God wanted to tell me that I would reach a ripe, old age and that my obituary would one day tell the story of a well-lived life, like his. Or maybe God wanted to remind me that angels are everywhere — acting through ordinary people like you and me — and that even when we are in the waiting room at the end of the world, we are never alone.

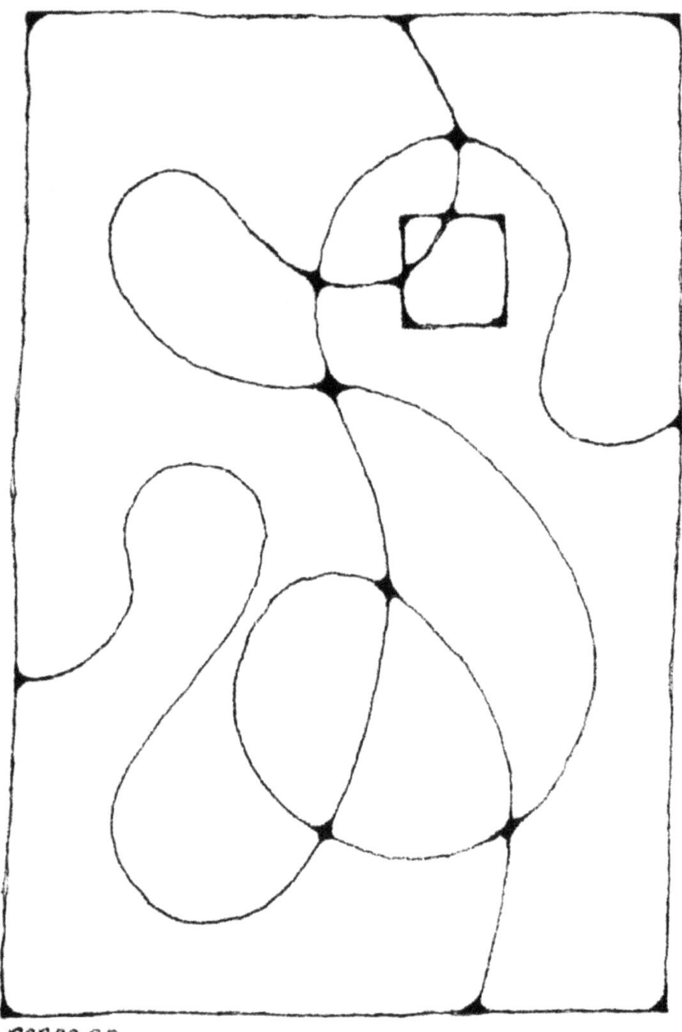

renee 55

What is a heart
Beyond a function of aliveness
A pumping existence
    A flow
      A validation?
It hurts
    Because of its wisdom
        Its compassion
          Its knowing
              That no matter what you think
                It knows better
                  And you know it
                      Even if you don't want to.
It fails
    To let us down easy
      To let us believe our story
          To let us distract our days
              For too long.
It speaks
    In the language of emotion
        Of sensual flesh and of rooted earth
            Of unbridled joy and visceral grief
                Of sloppy, organic authenticity
                  Of ancient whispers
                      Beyond words or letters
What is a heart
    But a doorway
      Into which
          Trembling, if we enter
              We will at last understand
                  How it keeps us alive.

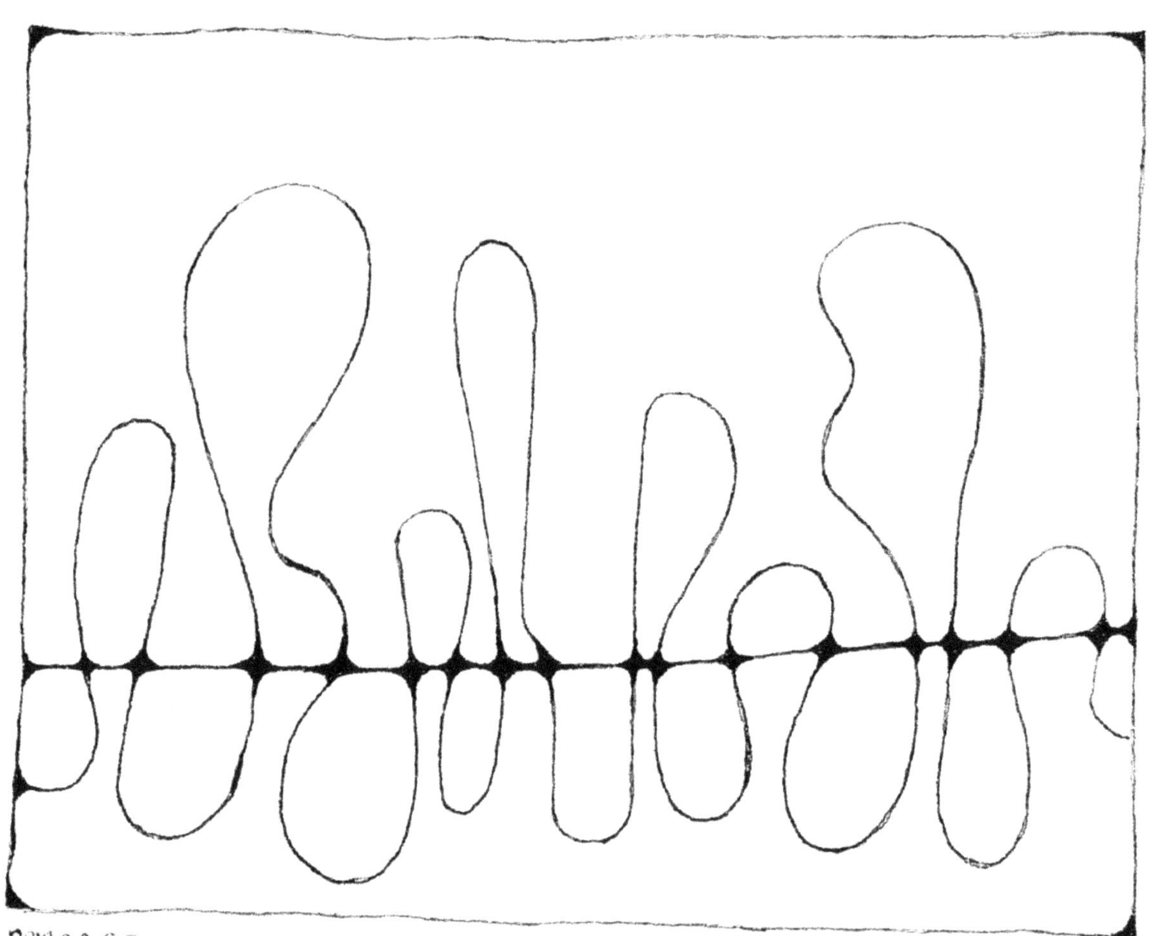

rence 85

Poem for Otto: Stuffed Cabbage

For many years
I lovingly devoured stuffed cabbage
made by Father on the kitchen counter in Connecticut.
My father learned how to make stuffed cabbage
from his mother,
when they grew up in the old country.
My senses are seduced.
The meat tempts my tongue,
the smell delights my nose,
steam rising from the warm meal
tempts my eyes,
I am no longer a child, my body,
my mind, and my spirit were deteriorating,
so I had my gall bladder removed.
My stomach is upset
when I sit at my father's kitchen table
eating stuffed cabbage:
my comfort food.
I am an adult
I am free to eat what I choose
I swallow a mouthful of regret,
while I choose to share a meal with Father
a meal that brings back many memories.

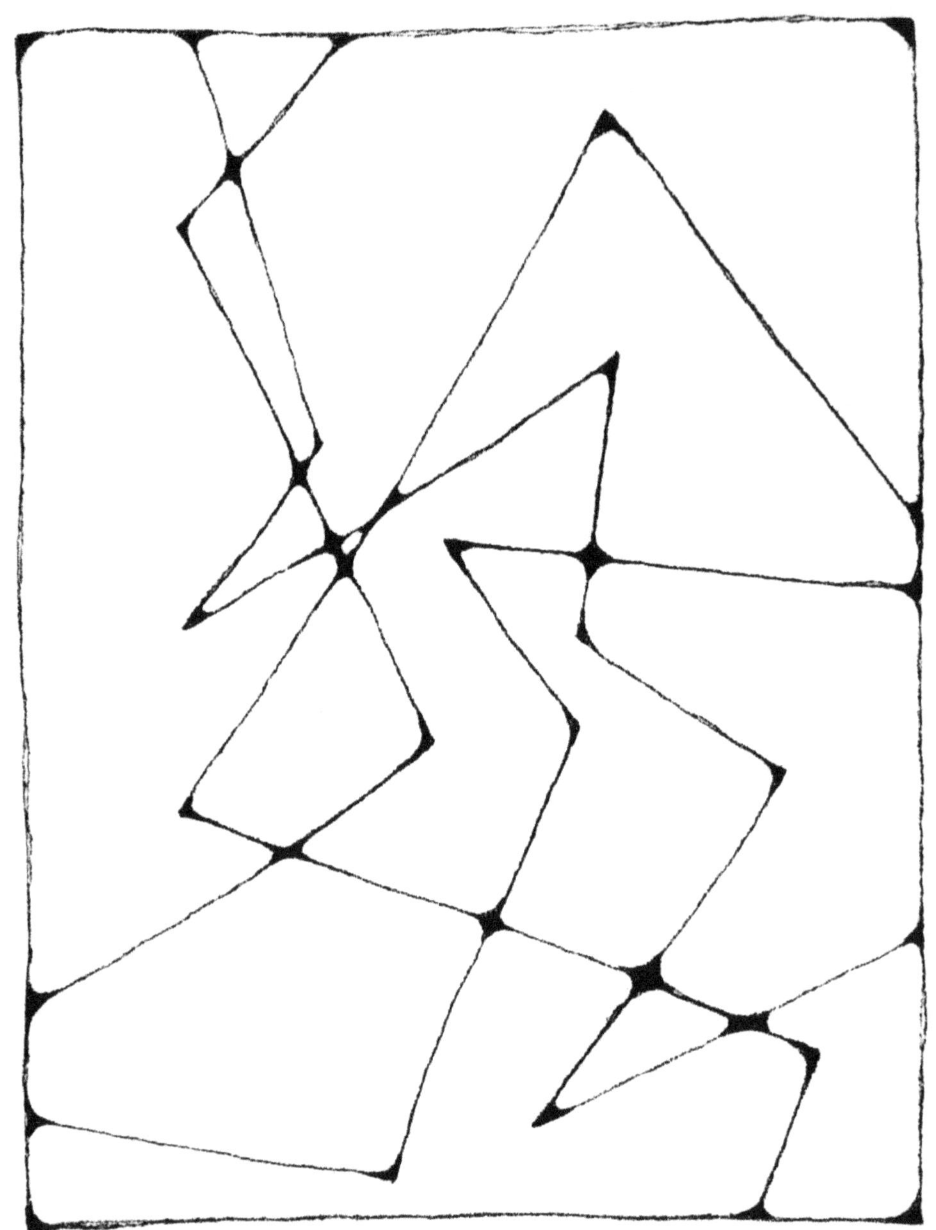

renee ss

My Flag, and Why July 4th is Important to Me

In 2009, I was approaching retirement with the Army, and felt I could not leave without going overseas to a combat zone. I found a unit out of St. Petersburg, Florida, that was slated to go to Iraq, and I submitted my name for consideration. Many months later, I found myself in Iraq with the 345th CSH (Combat Support Hospital). I was the Assistant Officer in Charge of the ED; I ran the night shift.

Life in the desert was not unlike the movie *MASH* to a certain extent. In the ED in a combat zone, it is either feast or famine. You are either endlessly watching movies of Andy Griffith, playing scoreless card games, working out, partaking of monotonous classes…or…you're going with no food, no sleep, no movies, and absolutely no time clock. And when it was busy, usually all Hell broke loose. It was controlled chaos at best. It was rare for us to get one wounded soldier at a time from a firefight. Usually, it was at least five, sometimes twelve. When this happened, the ED came alive, everyone knew their place, time was like a candle burning at both ends, and we didn't waste a second. In the year my unit was deployed in Iraq, we lost one soldier. Everyone else who managed to make it through our swinging doors lived.

Much bothered me about my deployment. As a nurse, there were no combat missions for me, no route clearances, no risk of sniper fire. Yet every day I would see soldiers mounted on their vehicles to go on mission, their game faces fixed to handle the unknown that lay ahead. Jokes were nervously told that were not that funny but brought loads of laughter to their companions. Their weapons were slung in odd configurations that best suited their personal preference. I felt that they were risking more, giving more, and after I watched them drive away, I would slowly turn and walk back into my safe, hard-shelled hospital and await their return. Except this time, I feared I would see them returning on a stretcher instead of in their vehicle.

Life continued like this for a while. One of the things we all did as individuals was to buy a flag and then have it flown over the camp in a Blackhawk helicopter during a mission. It was then signed by the pilot, and we would have our coveted combat flag to take home. I kept my flag in my cubby hole for a while. It sat in the back of the clinics in its airtight pouch for months.

One night, we got a call concerning a Special Forces Soldier who was shot under the arm while entering a house. He was coming in by chopper fast and hot. The soldier had his weapon up while entering a house, and the insurgent fired through a door opposite him. The bullet went over his body armor, into the armpit, through the heart, and exited out the other armpit. He was essentially dead when he got to us; he had all but bled out. We worked on him for 40 minutes. Only his physical conditioning and age had kept his broken heart beating this long, but his injuries were too great…and we lost him.

We had never lost a soldier before.

Some people walked away slowly, some did not hide their tears, others busied themselves by cleaning up, some showed anger, all seemed to carry away an unspoken weight that they would forever bear.

After about an hour, one of the Special Forces Team members came in to see their friend. He was visibly shaken and asked me if his friends could come in to pay their respects. His uniform was bleached yellow by the sun, his 14-day old beard was unkempt, and desert sand shook off his body with every step. As I stood there talking to him, I was regrettably aware of the crispness of my uniform – it was still white-grey camouflaged as if it had just been removed from the bag instead of having it for six months. My Green Beans coffee cup was just within his eyesight, and I was never so embarrassed. It seemed to glow like a miniature lighthouse, letting every real combat soldier know just how easy I had it. Here was a battle-hardened soldier who fought because he was called, and now he had lost his best friend…his battle buddy, we called them.

As much as I wanted to grant his request, we were a working ED in a combat zone, and the night was still young, and other wounded soldiers were expected. I told him with all the gentleness I possessed that I could not accommodate his request at this time. He bowed his head for a moment, and with a desperate, breaking voice he said, "Sir, surely there is someplace we can put him?" I stared at him for a moment. To see such a warrior humbly ask for something that we should have been prepared for – a casualty – was moving. Of course, we had mortuary affairs, but there was no actual place at night where he could be viewed. Suddenly, I remembered that I had the keys to the day clinic next door. It was used for minor non-emergent illness. I opened the clinic, placed the body inside, and circled the chairs around the dead hero. Still there was something missing, and I immediately knew what it was. I ran to the back of the ED behind the trauma bay and retrieved my flag out of my cubby hole. I then draped it over the body, and a soldier then took up his position at the head of the gurney. From that moment on, there would be someone assigned to this dead soldier, guarding him until he was placed into the ground at his place of burial in the U.S.

I learned several things that night. First, even though I would never kick in doors in search of the enemy, my battle raged all the same. My fight took place in a 10ft by 10ft square, and along with the doctors, nurses, and medics that served with me. We would give it everything we had and more to save our wounded soldiers…if we could. And finally, as I stood over in the corner quietly and watched the many soldiers file in and pay their last respects, I realized I had found the perfect place to hang my flag. Its golden tassels spanned the length of his body in perfect formation. It would never wave more gallantly than in its still position and could serve no better purpose than to be draped over the body of a fallen American soldier.

Johnny Masiulewicz

Unflowered

I.
considerably
heavier than hers, his bod-
y on the mattress
formed a slight depression in-
to which her body would roll

II.
the mouth is
unflowered

unflowering the
mouth only to heal, to inhale
from the cig, only to
mouth John Lennon lyrics

unflowering the
mouth only to pant
into another's mouth

III.
maybe once in a
while he should have slept through the
alarm clock. maybe
once in a while he should have
stayed in bed, slept in with her

IV.
the flower is removed
from the mouth only to heal,
to inhale from the cig, only
to mouth "Yes you can
radiate ev'rything you are"

continuously the tongue
scrapes gainst the
upper teeth. continuously,
til the tongue protrudes
permanently

the flower is removed
from the mouth only for
a cigarette drag, only
to pant into another's mouth

V.
maybe he should have
slept in. yes, that would have
healed ev'rything. that
would have. that would have. yes, that
would have. that maybe would have

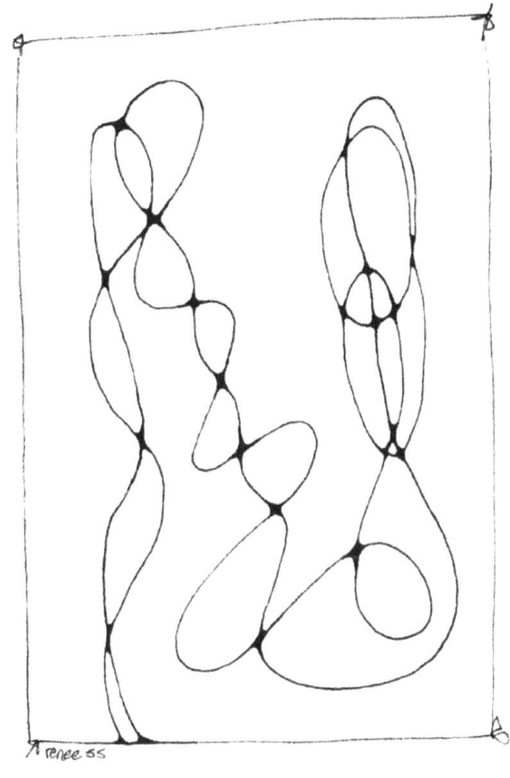

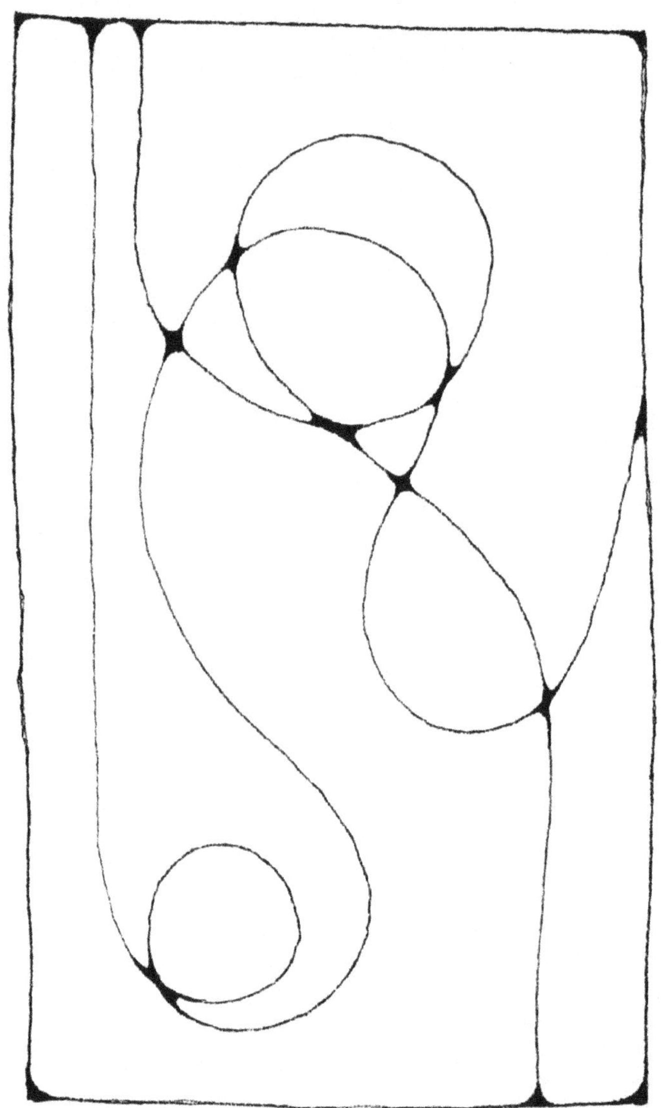

renee ss

It's My Senior Year!

I quivered with excitement as I woke up on the first day of my senior year of high school. Dances, parties, college applications, proms, and graduation were conjured with anticipation! On the afternoon of the first day, my father arrived home, looking weary. He glumly expressed, "Your mom had a radical mastectomy today. It was a long surgery. The lymph nodes in her arms were removed. She is in a lot of pain. You can go see her tomorrow." I exchanged glances with my brother. We were immobile. Then I rose like any other day and began to set the table. Dad took out the cast-iron skillet and prepared his favorite wiener stew. We ate in silence.

After dishes were done, I hugged my dad and brother and climbed the stairs to find the sanctuary of my room. My prayers were angry, and I just wanted to scream, "I am seventeen years old! This is my senior year! Why now?"

My sleep was fitful as fear and worry strangled my dreams. Somehow I woke up in time and ran to the bus stop. At school, the clock dragged each minute in slow motion, teachers mumbled, and my friends' voices buzzed. When I got home, I grabbed my guitar and drove to the hospital. Mom was lying in a bed. She was hooked up to machines and a monitor and had bandages across her chest. I embraced my misshapen, broken mother. To distract myself from the reality, I sang two songs I had written. Mom groggily replied, "Well, I guess you have talent."

"Yes, Mom, I really love to play the guitar." She smiled and soon fell asleep. I kissed her goodbye. On the way to the car, my anger was surging. Just scream! The scream and sobs started with, "But it is my senior year and now this! How will I have fun? How will my dream come true? Why, Mom, did this have to happen?"

Each day as I climbed the stairs to my room, I would pass Mom's bedroom. The door was closed. I could hear her sobbing, moaning, and pleading with God, "Why me? I am too young to die." Would my hugs be enough to console her? Hugs were all I had; words melted in the tears. She was forced to see the mastectomy scars every day in the mirror. She endured the chemo and retched in the bathroom. The wig and prosthesis were set on her dresser.

Senior year rolled forward with football games, Sadie Hawkins, Homecoming, and class musicals. This was the contrast to darkness in my home. By Christmas, Mom's cancer was in her lungs. My sister returned from college and faced Mom's changed image. She and I agreed to make this a happy Christmas. Mom helped us to decorate and make cookies. Was it going to be Mom's last Christmas? The cancer ravaged a path in Mom's body, metastasizing and destroying organs. She found strength to get dressed, and we celebrated my eighteenth birthday at a fancy restaurant. My wish, as I blew out the candle, was to have my mom with me forever.

Dad ordered a hospital bed to be placed in the dining room. My aunt left her five children in Louisiana and came to minister to my mom. Ladies from the church provided meals. I just muddled through each day, trying to find hope. By March, the cancer was in her brain, and she lost speech and mobility. The words were whispered, "Just a matter of time." On April 17 of my senior year, my friend Claire dropped me at my house. We chatted until I noticed my mom's best friend who was standing on the porch, motioning me to come. Miss Joan embraced me and tearfully said, "Your mom died at the hospital at 1:15 today."

But it was my senior year!

Where were the tears? After nine months of crying, the tears seem to have struck a dry well. We all went through the motions. Family arrived. The principal of my high school granted all of the seniors the day off to attend my mother's service. A smile was pasted on my face. The hugs were received, and words of comfort were spoken. The funeral procession was forty-two cars long, mostly comprised of my friends. After a few days, it was just my dad, my brother, and me facing our grief.

But it was my senior year! Prom, Senior Ditch Day, graduation, and parties filled my schedule. On Graduation Day, as I crossed the stage, I glanced into the audience. Four hundred and fifty students were giving me a standing ovation. My senior year was finished. Now, my path as a motherless child was beginning. I staggered in the tunnel of grief, groping for a smidgen of hope.

reneess

Lately, it has seemed that…

Every man who takes me out is already taken
What is it about me
Do I give off side-chick vibes
Do I come across as easy to please
And is it no wonder I write stories
About the end of the world
With my emotional apocalypse happening
On the regular because

Every man who takes me out is already taken
It takes a while for the truth to come out
They are testing the waters
Looking to see what else is out there
I am the shiny, sparkly thing that catches their eye
I am smiling and grateful for the attention
I am nice when I find out the truth
I go quietly, I do not give them away when

Every man who takes me out is already taken
Their wives or girlfriends or fiancées
Come along in the changing path of their shadows
The best first-date question:
"Is there anyone who believes they are in
A relationship with you right now?"
I always forget to ask
I do not need to because I should know by now

Every man who takes me out is already taken
This is the reality we live in now
Too many choices and too many options
Why not explore them all
Who can it hurt if you just dip your foot in
Then pull it back and go on your way
Buy your girl some flowers she thinks
Are for no reason at all
When they were ripped stem by stem
From my skin

Facebook Post, August 2023

I got to the beach an hour before sunrise. Orion hung low in the sky. At the horizon, Venus pulsed solid with her love.

Today I found a solitary bench facing the water. I stood on it.

In the dark, alone, I began dancing without music, letting the off-shore breeze dictate my moves. As my arms drifted like wild tree moss in the salty air, I did an homage to my fierce and feral lover. Freedom is his name. Abusive and harsh, yet tender and kind, I welcome him. For he is exactly what I've asked for.

Like a mad woman, I have been riding this vibrant beast through the passages of my life. Barebacked, I am tossed in ecstatic motion again and again, clinging to his ephemeral fur with only a faint hope of stability.

Still dancing to the rising sun, I picture Freedom running me deeper and deeper into the wilderness. Alone…alone...together we wander his liminal land.

At the deepest, darkest part of the forest, he pauses. Still panting heavily from our wild ride, I hear him whisper in my ear, "Find your way home, sweet one."

And he's gone.

Somehow, with no map, no guide...just a single star, I find myself back here on the bench, at the beach, comforted by the eternal return of the rising sun.

I move and twist and spin and write to you now, and I feel *him* here. Freedom licks my wounds, plays with my hair, smiles tenderly, and laughs, "I never really left you."

I kiss my lover's cheek and thank him for the ride. And I continue to dance,

      sipping life,

         sleeping with shadows,

            awakening my immortal coil…

               …awestruck and baffled by it all.

HOPE

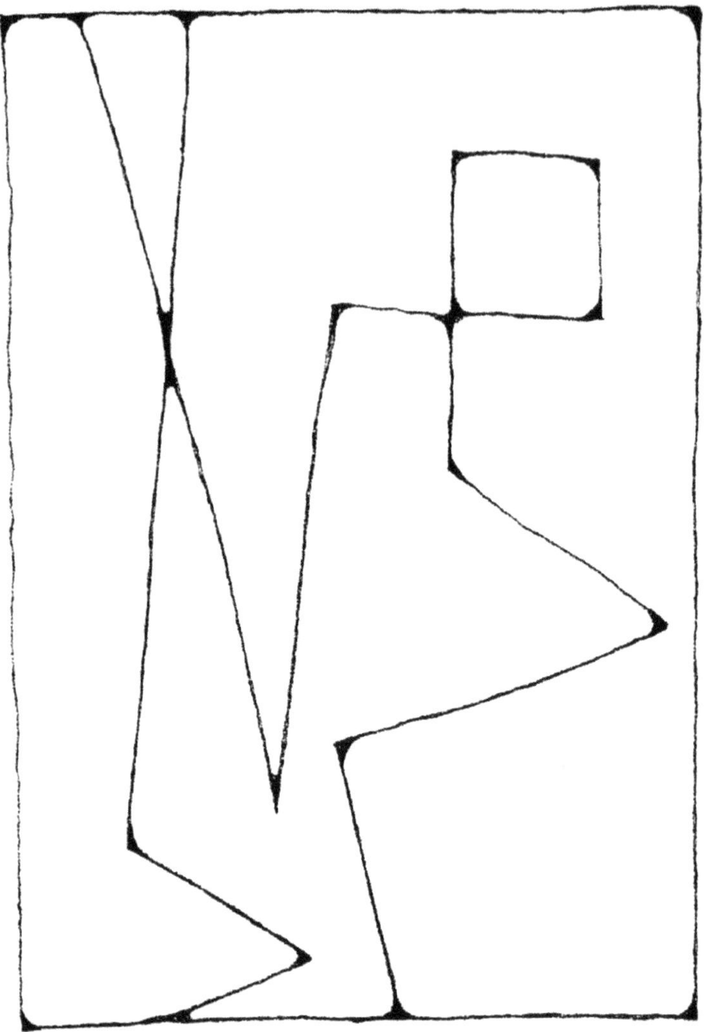

renee ss

Silver Linings

Growing up, our mom always told us what she wanted most in life was to be a mother. She raised us on her own, and we were extremely close. So, when my brother passed away just before his tenth birthday, it left just her and me. We were wounded and tender but found the strength we needed to persevere in each other. She was my touchstone; I was her hope. We moved through this world together as a unit – our bond fortified in mutual strength. We learned together, played together, and made most of life's big decisions together.

So at just 26, when I was faced with the harsh reality of her sudden death, it forced a shift in me that permeated all aspects of my life and forever redefined my person. The first phase of the shift began just a few hours after learning the news. I was on the phone with my aunt, and she was speaking to me as if I was an adult. Even in my mid-twenties, in my family dynamic I still felt like one of the children. I had been through quite a bit of death before, but all of the *what comes next?* minutiae was always taken care of by the "grown-ups," which I didn't fully appreciate until the horrifying gut punch that this now included me.

My immediate family was always just the two of us – until it wasn't. I had never felt so incredibly alone. And, instead of leaning on my Mom for guidance, to which I was accustomed, I was suddenly an integral part of making decisions about how to say goodbye to her. The circumstance was surreal, and the roar of its injustice was deafening.

But, every dark cloud does indeed have a silver lining, the magnificence of which can be life changing. My silver linings have significantly shaped the subsequent phases of my life.

Beyond rocking my world emotionally, my mother's untimely passing also produced great positive change for me.

When you grow up being one part of a two-person team, you tend to view life from a united-front standpoint. We had all we needed in each other and never really ventured out of our personal fortress of solidarity. Our invisible tether connected us to one another, no matter where we were. This bond lent itself to a sort of co-dependent independence, which I had to learn to navigate away from. The security of her earthly presence was a force that made me feel safe and grounded. Without it, I had to find a way to be that force for myself. My mom's passing taught me how to truly stand on my own two feet. Over time, I've also come to realize the inherent strength in connecting with other human beings for help and guidance – and to no longer view this as weakness.

As death often does, hers infused me with an urgency to live – *more*. My wife recognized this primal need and agreed to move three states away to be closer to my best friend and extended family. With nothing more to guarantee our success than a desperate grip on the notion that we would *leap and the net would appear*, we uprooted our lives in search of the something missing.

The courage such a huge transformation took imbued me with a strength that has fueled me ever since. I felt strong in my ability to adapt to change – even when the outcome was uncertain. And, I learned to embrace my newly independent life – without the cushion of the sounding board I had been so accustomed to relying on.

Part of what makes this human experience so remarkable is the influence others have on it. I have felt the permanence of my mother's significance in every moment since her death and found a strength in myself that I could have only found without her.

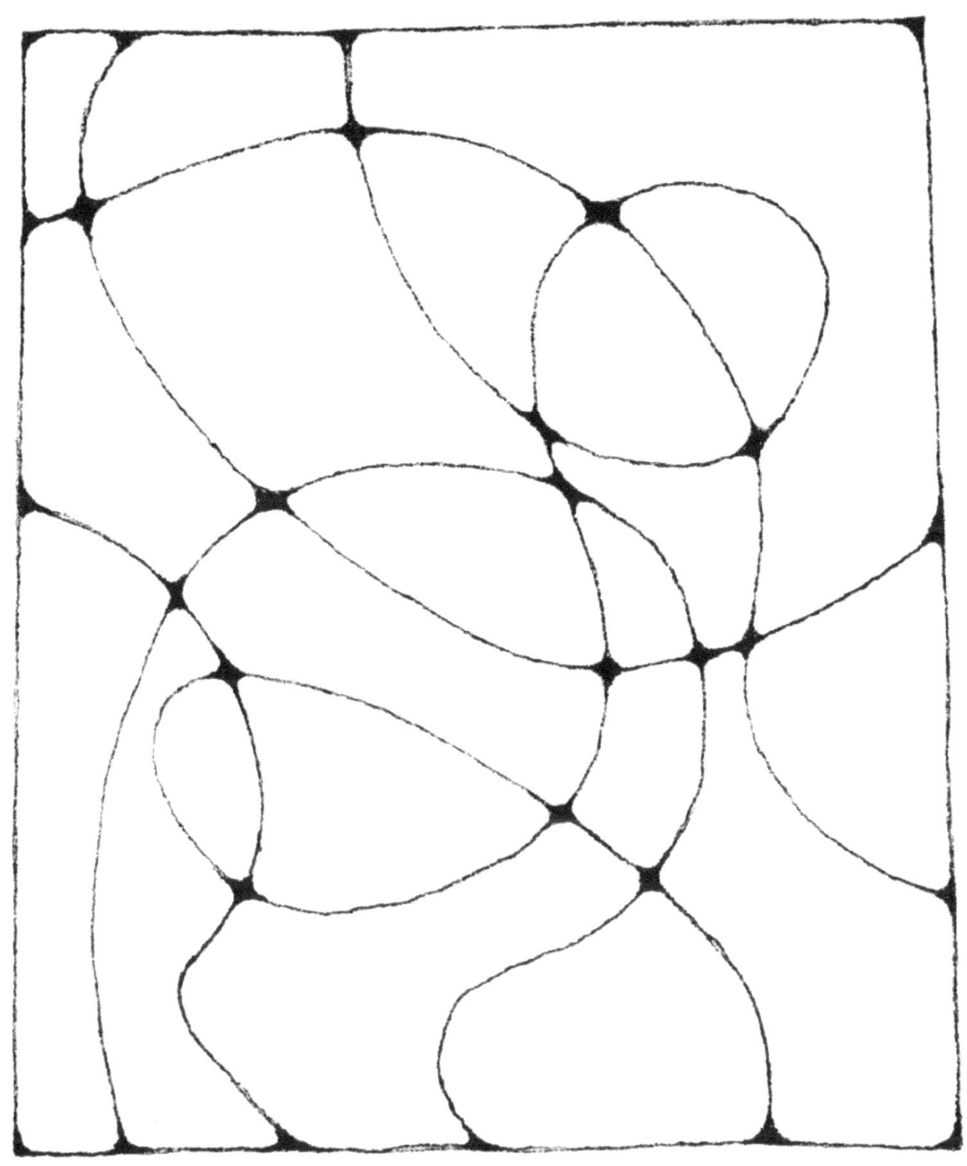

renee ss

Facebook Post, July 2023

I've been working my way through so many things in these past few years, taking an ax to the stalagmites and stalactites I've built up over the years in the corners of my mind. Those thoughts of unworthiness, those habits of devaluing myself. You know, all the fun stuff so many women especially pick up along the way.

Losing my cheerleader, the guy who regularly drained the grease trap, forced me into some heavy lifting. I've been sitting with my pens and my journals, and my faith and perspective, most mornings and writing my way to freedom, to "better mental health," lol. When I cross over, if my kids read my journals, they'll find all the beautiful clues I was given along the way, all the doors that were gently eased open for me by Spirit, or Shirley, or whatever language you want to use to describe Love. Certainly not every morning do I find manna but often enough to keep me out there searching the skies.

Yesterday's lesson was about timing. I picked up a book of prayers I've been reading through and asked specifically for a gift on Paul's birthday. And then I randomly opened up to this page, "The Perfect Mate." Ha! That Shirley is quite the celestial prankster. But the story was actually about timing.

If I celebrate and give thanks for the timing of Paul coming into my life, of the ways we helped rescue each other and discover life together, and I do…if I trust that timing, and I do…then don't I have to trust the timing of his leaving? I can't cherry-pick the plan, celebrate only the good, the fun, the things I perceive immediately as gifts, and then discard the rest. Either I believe or I don't. Either my life has unfolded as a precious gift of care and love and personalized beauty, or it hasn't. I dunno…it helped me yesterday. As did the gatherings of friends who reached out or came around me yesterday. Turned out to be a great day, a day that Paul may have loved seeing. I hope so.

Today I'm back at it, pickax in hand. Chiseling away the untruths, the hurtful habits, and exposing the thick veins of joy and beauty in the walls, buried beneath. Thankful for the Light, and for the ways y'all share it so beautifully. ☺☺☺

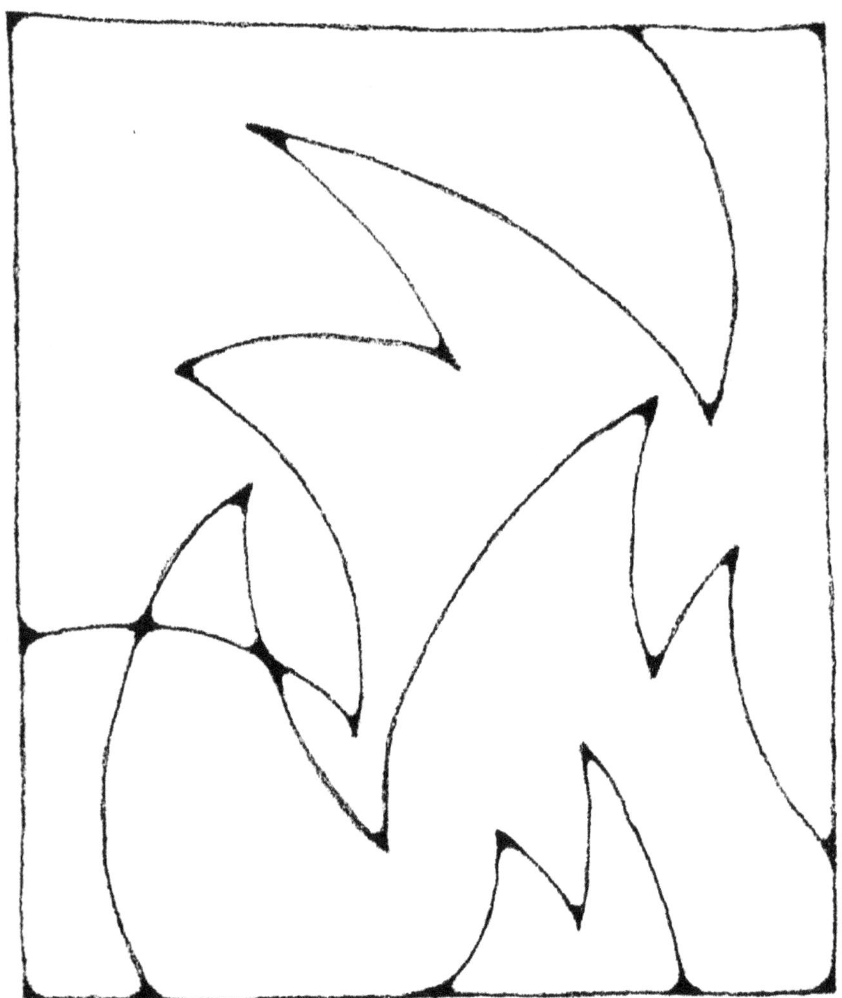

renee SS

Consolation Prize

Banshee winds tore the roof off my house and left her delicate innards exposed for all the world to see.

Now, fine drops of silty water ran down the flanks of my Grandma's bronze horse lamps. The woman never rode a horse in her life, but these two lamps had been among her most prized possessions. Their once creamy-white silk shades now bore streaks of black attic dust at least one hundred and fifty years old.

At first, no tarps big enough to cover the gaping hole where the roof once sat could be found. So, rain water had poured straight down the inside walls all the way to the ground floor unchecked for hours.

Standing in the hallway, I could envision the damp meeting dormant fungi spores, lurking deep within the walls, greedily embrace one another and begin to form some great black creeping thing that would soon coat the hidden insides of her smooth plaster walls.

The great old house had proudly perched at the top of Main Street, held aloft by her fifteen brick pillars for as long as anyone here could remember. Now, with her roof shorn clean off, the old girl looked more like a squatty toad than the graceful swan she once was. Like a woman who has just lost her all of her hair.

"She's a goner," Rick Elwood, my insurance man, said, sadly shaking his head as he stood beside me, peering up at the startling blue tarps that now billowed and snapped in the breeze. "Take the check and move on," he suggested, his kind grey eyes meeting mine. "You'll never be able to make her livable again. You'd have to tear down the walls to the studs to get rid of the mold, and that'll cost a fortune.

"You'll get a good amount of money for that heart pine inside, if you have her taken down.

Take the money, go live the life you deserve somewhere else, Lorelai." He used my whole name. Not the nickname that had been tacked onto me since I was a small child, Lore.

Rick was my age; we had gone to high school together. I never paid any mind to him back then. I was held captive by the glow that was Bill.

The brilliant sun shining through vivid blue plastic bathed everything below in a watery blue glaze. Even in his tinted-blue state, it was clear to me now just how very tall and handsome Rick Elwood was. He was a widower now, missing a spouse, like me.

He knew about Bill. The whole town knew about Bill and his short-skirted secretary. My brain fog obscured her name for a moment. Something like chenille, was that it? Cheryl, Cherie, Sherelle? Shaney – there it was. Shaney Boothe. The woman was all legs and teeth with a glossy brown mane. Her Hollywood name would surely be Sha-Boo. If she lived in Hollywood.

She was one of those people who never seemed to look exactly the same in any photograph. Like she might be a totally different person in every single image. My Bill, dazzled and snatched away from me by a shapeshifter.

Rick was still talking, but I had drifted away again. Something I was prone to do these days.

"Salvage what you can," he was saying. "Go out west for a while. Doesn't Emma Jean live in L.A. now?

My brilliant girl had done well for herself. She was indeed living in Los Angeles, making a name for herself writing snappy one-liners for a wildly popular, but too smutty in my opinion, sitcom.

She now went by E. J. Wills instead of the name we had given her, Emma Jean Wilkins. And she was and always would be a daddy's girl. She didn't want to hear me out about her daddy and She-Boo. How he had humiliated me by having a torrid affair right under my nose.

After thirty years of marriage. Wanting a divorce so he could marry Shady Long Legs and live happily ever more in glorious bliss. Until a few years from now, when the hussy will inevitably find herself yet another handsome older man. One with more money than Bill. One she can sink those teeth into.

"It happened, Mama," Emma had said. "Sometimes things happen, and you need to accept it and move on."

Sweet girl, I wanted to tell her, *I hope one day when you finally meet that perfect person, your other missing piece, that you never have to understand what moving on truly means*. This poor old bald-headed house was the last thing left that I could truly call my own. Left to me by my sweet grandma. Packed to the roof with family treasures – dated, useless, but fervently clutched to the bosoms of all the women who had dwelled within these walls for decades.

I could break free now, though. Here was a thing to consider. I was still young enough, at least in my head, to have a bit more fun. I was done with Bill. Even though he had been the love of my life, I would never again be able to picture him in the same golden light I'd always drawn around him.

I won't even keep the horse lamps. Sell it all. Let the whole town squelch across my grandma's pastel rugs. Pick and choose what they will. I will take their money along with their pretend sympathy smiles. Whispered tittle-tattle. And then I'll take down the house, so she can live on with dignity as someone else's very expensive living-room floors. So she doesn't have to anchor here for years, gradually falling in on herself.

Then, I'll find a new place. Not the west coast, but someplace Emma might want to come and visit. Maybe even stay for weeks at a time.

I brushed a wisp of my thinning hair away from my eyes.

"Rick, have you ever been to Hawaii?

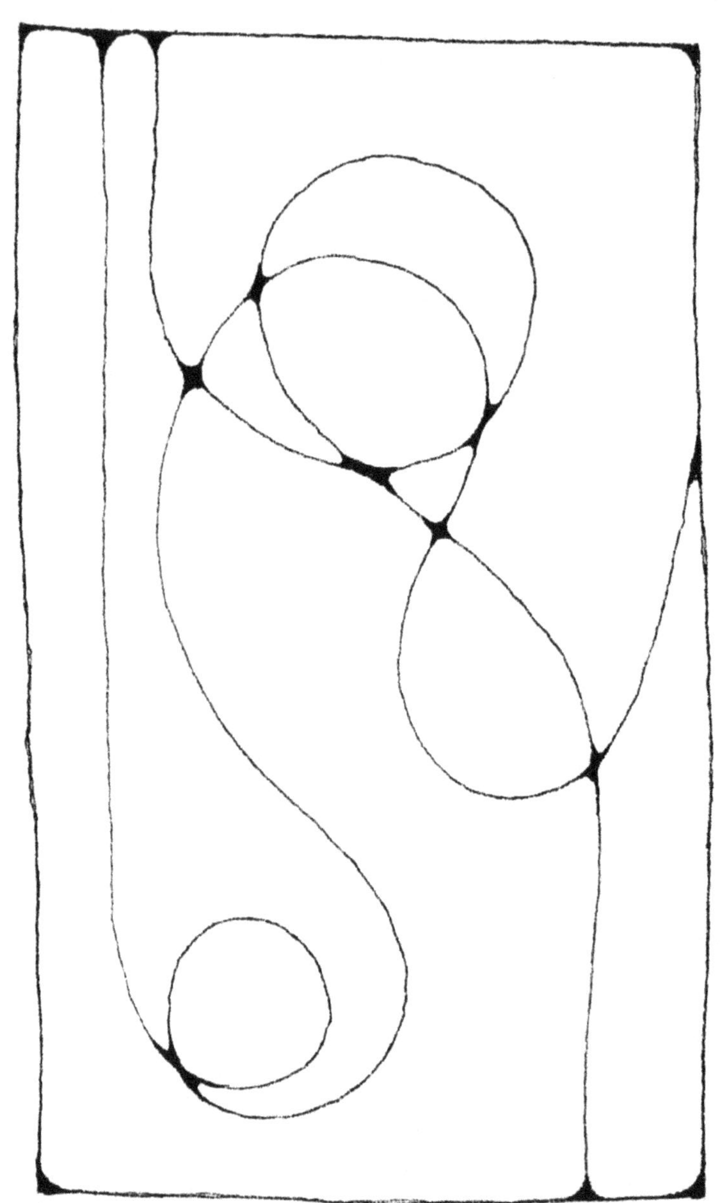

renee ss

Hope Is Not a Plan...

Back during one of my restaurant gigs, I used to wait on a guy whose favorite two expressions were "hello contains no information" and "hope is not a plan." He was much more pleasant than these statements might imply; he was just more of a "brass tacks" kind of guy. The first statement made sense to me, especially if answering a phone in some work capacity. The second statement I would debate in my head while wandering back to the bar to pick up his Scotch with two ice cubes. Not one. Not three. Two.

This weekend, "hope is not a plan" came to mind two different times. I got to spend some fun time with school friends, and it came up as part of an amicable discussion of politics, action, and the value of messaging.

The next day, I ran into another woman from school I had not seen in 20 years, and we chatted a bit in the grocery store. In response to my comments on the passage of time, she began discussing just how awful the world had become, that life was so much better when we were young. I started discussing why I felt hopeful, perhaps as more of a shield to what she was saying, but I was also earnest in my desire to remind her of reasons to consider hope.

This morning, I watched an episode of *A Small Light*—a scene where Miep Gies gives the young Anne Frank a dress and a pair of shoes and tells her that she will need them one day for job interviews and other adult pursuits. It's a lovely scene of a young woman feeling the joy of maturation, underscored by what we all know will be the tragic reality to come.

Yet that gift meant so much to both giver and receiver, as a visioning of what might be, what they looked forward to after the war. The thread of hope pulling them through was mightier than it might have seemed, as it was often their only choice if they were to see another day.

I realize now that my capacity for hope was a gift. Perhaps not a plan, but it was one of the instruments by which I came through a difficult period of youth when I was bullied, often living in the shadows of a stormy household that knew addictions and regret. Hope was how I entertained myself, how I committed to somehow helping my family through their tough times, how I knew, absolutely knew, life would get better.

Is hope appropriate in our current context? This age of partisan battles, this age of grievance? So many of us want to acknowledge the wrongs of the past, but how do we do so without bitterness overtaking us? Is hope entertained by our forebearers something we need to treat as a family heirloom? Do we use it to live lives worth their hard work and sacrifices? Is hope truly a means of traveling?

Next month, while in Amsterdam, I will be visiting the Anne Frank Museum, and I suspect the experience will bring a mixture of emotions. My husband would not be going if I had not insisted; it's not something one thinks of doing as part of a "holiday." I told him that Anne Frank was someone who had shown me the power of the written word. Despite how her story ended, her story is never ending. Her voice of hope was too strong to remain silent, and she has reminded us all to be our best selves, to believe that we can be noble in our pursuits and our daily lives.

Hope may not be a plan but is often a choice. We often say that life is a series of choices, conscious and unconscious. Fortunate are those who find it easy to choose patience and hope, and glory to all of us who do not wish to destroy it, no matter how hard it is to believe in it.

That is a form of hope, as well — something that might be divine within our humanness.

Soul Diving

She never thought she could,
She never thought she would.
She didn't even know how.
But then it happened
And... without thinking,
She stepped up.
She found her way.
She did it
Because she could,
Because she should,
Because it was in her.
It had always been in her.
It was who she was
even when she didn't know.
You have it, too.
I see it in your eyes.
It rests in your heart,
Ready for when you need it.
Believe in yourself
And you will find...
Your strength.

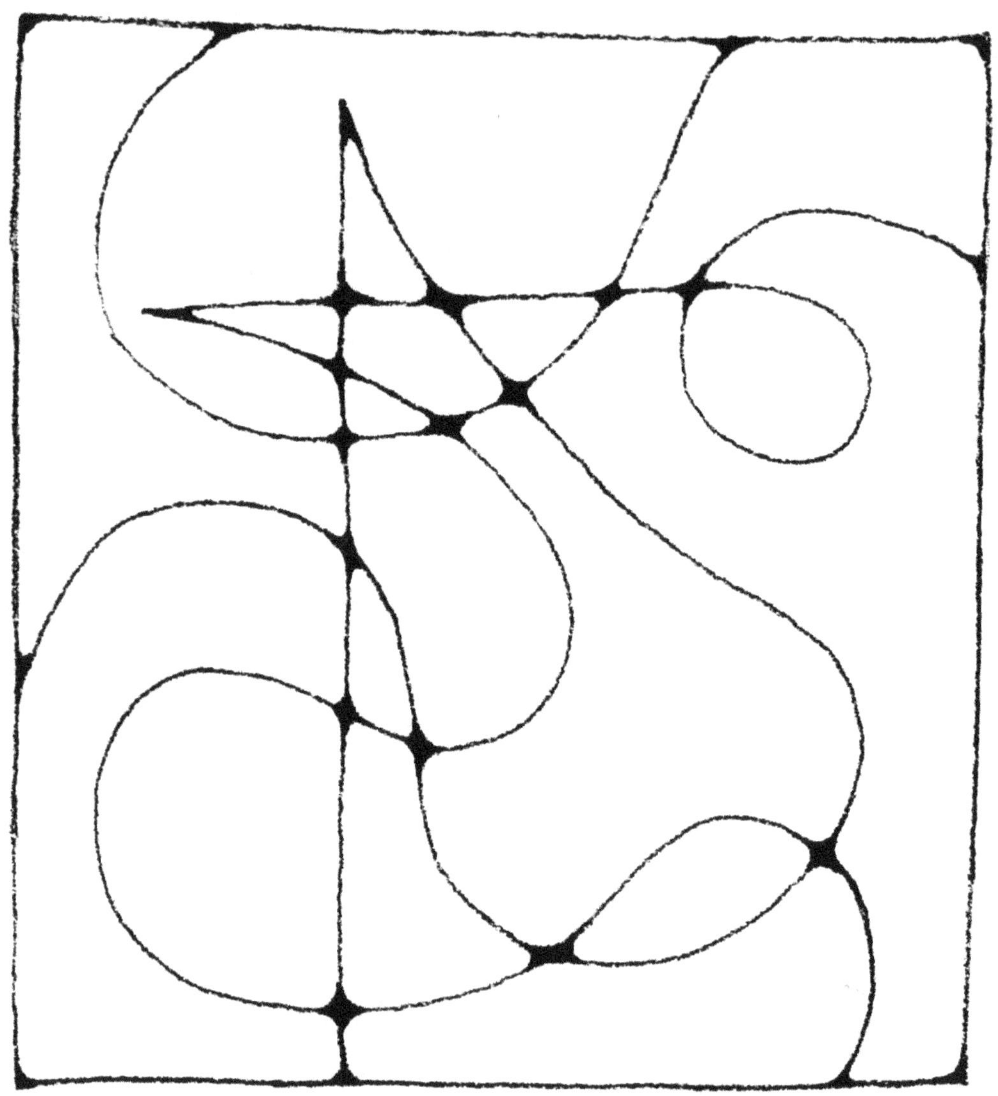

renee ss

My Love Letter to Healing

"I'm leaving." I peeked my head in the kitchen doorway. His broad shoulders, back facing, expressed no emotion but a release of tension.

It was over; his fight for us was over. My fight was over.

"As much as it hurts…" I began to reply to his silence. I sat down the suitcase. "I think it is for the best." Still he did nothing. Twenty-three years, and he acted as if I wasn't even there.

I gathered my belongings, tears rolling down my cheek, and turned away from my children's father — the man I thought I would grow old with, the one I built a home with, said my vows to — to step into a life I knew nothing about. As I retreated from our home, I pulled out the gently folded letter I had tucked under my arm and dropped it onto his recliner. I exhaled. I had no choice but to walk out the door, taking nothing but my clothes and the beautiful memories of what was.

"I left you something," I said, paying it forward as I entered my healing journey.

Dearest Healing,

I am sorry I pushed you away, so sorry I did not acknowledge how badly I needed you. Not only did you suffer, but those closest to you did as well, including myself. I thought I could maneuver through this life without you. You always said I was stubborn like that. Today I vow that I will make you my top priority. I know you lost your trust in me; I cannot blame you. I completely ignored you when you spoke, and I treated you like you did not even exist. I just continued living, without believing we could enjoy a life together. Instead of facing you head on, the pain blinded me. I am here now to change all of this, fight for our love — for us.

Oh, healing, I am at my darkest…

I have searched for you in all the places we used to go. I tried to find you in pleasing others. All I found was heartache and a feeling of unworthiness.

I need you more than ever…

We can take it slow. I will sit with you in silence and discomfort. One day at a time, one hour, one minute if that is what it takes. By our own rules. It is not going to be easy, especially on my part. I will stay determined and dedicated. I did not mean to run from you…

We can start out walking in nature, always your favorite place to be. You can teach me there. You always enjoyed the beach; we can hold hands and glance at our footprints to reassure each other that we are still together.

I will take you on adventures, romantic dinners, and a night out to see our favorite band play. You always loved to dress up. If you are up to it, we can meet up with friends and go to social events. I will buy you flowers and compliment you on how beautiful you are becoming. It will be just me and you — our rules!

We will pray, meditate, do therapy, whatever it takes to bring us closer together. We will earn the life of our dreams. I will stay completely dedicated to building a life with you.

We might lose people and material things not serving us. Detachment to who we once were. We will cry a thousand times, gripping each other every second until it passes. We will lose our appetite, not only for food but for our connection to the outside world. We will grab each other by the arm and force a conversation with a stranger, a healthy meal upon our lips. We shall never speak ill of one another, but we will caress each other's wounds and adore each passing second. We will struggle from time to time. Bliss, ecstasy, and wonderful adventures will await us. I am yours, and you are mine.

Love,

Me

Sometimes in life we expect people or things to make us happy, give all the expectations to ourselves. The day I truly began to heal, I pledged to move forward with resilience. We all long to receive beautiful love letters — and healing. So why not write one to yourself!

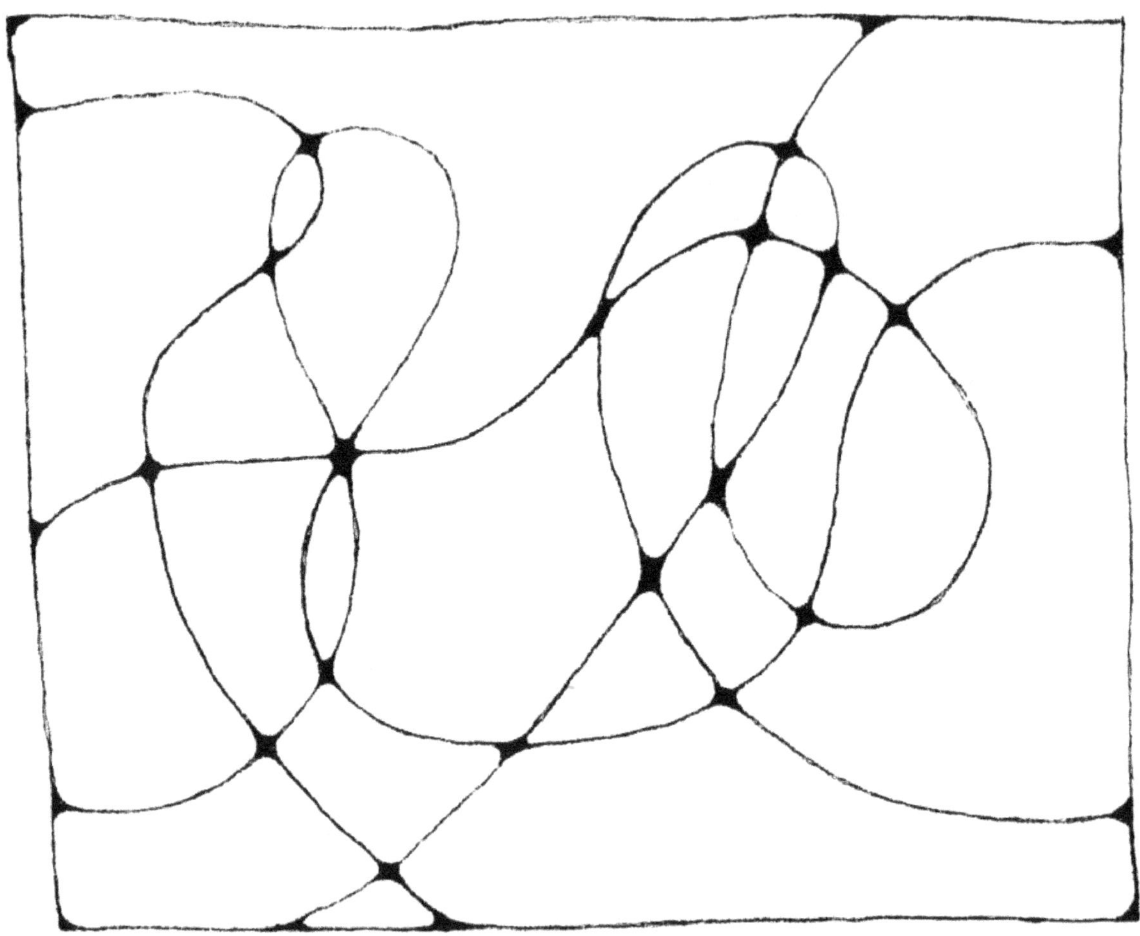

renee ss

Learning To Heal

Can't tell left from right,
Oh it ain't a pretty sight,
When the nut comes loose from behind the wheel.
Watching my life become a metaphor,
For every disappointment I've endured,
Now I'm learning to heal. Learning to heal.

I'm sure some of you can relate,
At attempts to self-medicate,
Using anything I could beg, borrow, or steal.
But foolishness can't remove the grief,
Or give my soul much relief,
So I'm learning to heal. Learning to heal.

An event void of reverie,
A simple quiet homecoming,
Giving my self-permission to be whole.

A smile can quickly become a frown,
When your whole world's turned upside down,
A foolish twist on hey — Let's Make A Deal.
Yet the past simply ain't gonna change,
No matter how much I complain,
So I'm learning to heal. Learning to heal.

So for now I must press on,

Anything less would just be wrong,
Take the time to figure out how I feel.
Maybe find the chance to catch a breath,
And a new definition of success.
Yeah I'm learning to heal. Learning to heal.

A Note from the Artist – Renee Simpson

Resilience….it is how I have survived…it is how we survive!!!
Paint it….what would it look like….what substrate…color…shape…..
It is simple and straightforward and I see an abstracted version….just line and in black and white….it's just that….black and white…. No in between….a definite decision. Also with a neurographic style which turns the corners…..resilience for me has been a lot of hitting the corner or the edge and smoothing it out to move on.

It's a journey that requires
.determination
.deliberate action
.presence
.courage
.open mindedness
.BOUNDARIES

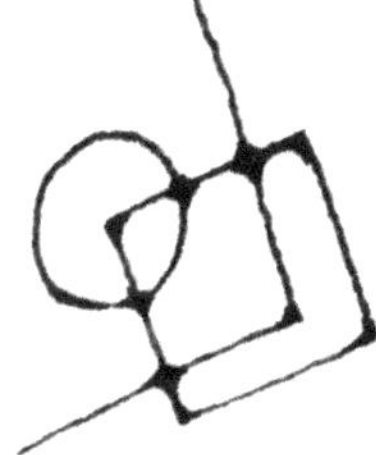

There is a power in resilience….survival and growth!

Here's to moving forward with resilience!

Renee Simpson has been painting wildly since the early 1990s. Her work has appeared in galleries all over the country, featuring a style that ranges from whimsical to soulful.
www.reneesimpson.art

About the Contributors

Ally Pfeifer composed her story a few months after her "Final Bow"—a graduation performance from Seminole State College's music program in 2012. She was born and raised in Central Florida but moved to Colorado Springs in June 2022. She owns a small business teaching voice and piano lessons to kids and teens, and she co-owns a photography company with her partner, Chase. www.chaseandally.com

Anastasia Forrest is a lifelong learner, creative, and sobriety-enthusiast based in St. Augustine, Florida. She has two amazing daughters and an awesome husband who builds beautiful houses. Anastasia works as a Real Estate Broker Associate with EXP Realty. Her creative passions are songwriting, authoring books, and painting. Her favorite things to do with her family are to go on vacations together. www.anastasiaforrest.com

Bob Pritchard is not interested in genres. What he does like is a good story told well. An avid reader, he grew up on Dickens, Tolkien, Hemmingway, and King. Classics, fantasy, horror or comedy, he has always been drawn, first and foremost, to good writing. So, when he started writing, he did not consider categories, just interesting characters and satisfying endings. Bob is the author of *Her Puerto Rican Smile* and the upcoming releases *The Man Who Wanted to be Cary Grant*, *The Man Who Wanted to be Tom Brady,* and the epic fantasy novel *The Silver Paladin*. He is currently working on a detective mystery novel. www.amazon.com.au/Her-Puerto-Rican-Smile-Pritchard/dp/B0CD8YW85B

Chris Bodor is a first-generation American. He was born in Connecticut to an English mother and a Hungarian father. During the past three decades, his poems have appeared in many independent, small, and micro-press publications, such as the *Lummox Journal, Live Nude Poems*, and *New Generation Beats: National Beat Poetry Foundation, Inc. 2022 Anthology*. He is currently serving a two-year term as the Florida State Beat Poet Laureate (2023-

2025). Bodor is the editor-in-chief of the international literary journal *A.C. PAPA*, which stands for Ancient City Poets, Authors, Photographers, and Artists. He lives and works in St. Augustine, the Nation's Oldest City.

Connie Helena is a Generation X writer and artist who self-published her first collection of writing, *The Green Orchid*, as she glided gently into the second century of her life. She is currently at work on a science fiction novel—a prequel and sequel to her short story "The Last Violence"—as well as a volume of poetry entitled *Journal of 1000 Days*. https://linktr.ee/conniehelena

Crystal Taylor specializes in working with consciousness via quantum trance. Quantum trance allows you to hear your own soul speak, thus allowing you to receive healing and get answers about your life. Crystal has performed groundbreaking work with quantum trance, where individuals have successfully channeled other souls to receive information about changes happening on Earth. www.quantumpriestessrealm.com

Debra Weller is an experienced early childhood educator and professional storyteller. She is a creative performance artist with over forty years' experience using oral-tradition storytelling to engage her audiences and students. Debra has told stories at festivals and events in the USA and internationally. She recently was chosen to perform at the 2023 Marrakech International Storytelling Festival and the Orlando Fringe. Debra trains professionals to use storytelling to enhance dynamic presentations. www.linktr.ee/debrawstoryteller and www.story-tellingcourses.com

Harold George has always been a people watcher and believes this habit has provided him with all the tools he needed to travel through life. The youngest of six sons, Harold was born in Minnesota and grew up in St. Augustine, Florida. With degrees in theater, communications, and library science, all of Harold's interests stem from his curiosity about the fascinating experience called human behavior. Writing has provided a process by which to understand the road traveled and a way to remind those around him that they matter so much more than they realize.

Janet Giese: "I started my career in fashion with the opening of my own boutique before moving into interior design and renovation. Along the way, my inner artist called me. My first focus was with paper sculpting and painting, before realizing that writing was in my soul. I have started several novels and have written children's books and one-paragraph stories, but my biggest love is poetry."

Johnny Masiulewicz is the author of the poetry collections *Keywords: A Dada_Experiment* and *Professional Cemetery,* and creator of the award-winning *Happy Tapir* zine series. His work has appeared in a variety of literary journals, on sites, and in anthologies including *Curbside Review, The Main Street Rag, Third Wednesday, Ash & Bones,* and *The Alembic.* A native Chicagoan, he now lives and works in Jacksonville, Florida.

Jorja DuPont Oliva is a multi-genre published author, beginning with her debut series, Chasing Butterflies, in 2013. She published her award-winning psychological thriller *Sisterly* in 2017 and her award-winning children's book *Mr. Dawg—I am a Frog* in 2020. Jorja also is a contributing author for multiple anthologies. In 2023, Jorja continues to write, with works in progress to include her first foray into historical fiction and a nonfiction self-health book.

Keith A. Rea—singer/songwriter, instrumentalist—brings a wealth of experience to the stage as well as a variety of styles and genres. From love songs to train songs, Keith's lyrics conjure stories of people, places, and situations that feel both familiar and yet somehow fresh. His instrumental stylings cover the landscape from finger-picked ballads to raucous twelve bar blues. www.keithrea.com

Kevan Breitinger is a woman who has been healed by words, freed by words, and whose spirit has always been quickened by words. It is the happiest of accidents that she also thoroughly enjoys writing them, for her own amusement and hopefully the pleasure of others, as well.

Kevin Cox was a New York City Police Officer and member of the Honor Legion of that department. In his career, he made over 500 arrests. After retiring his talents of finding those who didn't want to be found, and when making people come with him who didn't want to became stalking and kidnapping, he decided to write books instead. He is the author of a number of books, including *A Year in Bushwick* and *Back in Bushwick.*

Mark E. Hayes is a retired chemist who is now termed a Renaissance man. He moved from Indiana to China and became an actor. He was a feature writer for Shanghai publications and traveled extensively in Asia. The surf, sea, and sand engage his wild side. He samples languages, adores animals, and loves Italy. Mark lives in Northern Georgia with his wife, Vicki, and an unruly rescue dog.

Nancy Quatrano loves a mystery to read or to write, but poetry and short stories are where she started. She writes the award-winning Point and Shoot Mystery Series and co-authors the Amazing Grace Trucking Company series as N. L. Quatrano. She's on the board of the Florida Writers Foundation, which provides grants to promote literacy in underserved communities throughout Florida. www.nlquatrano.com

Nicole Linssens lives in beautiful North Carolina with her wife, daughter, and two dogs. She has a bachelor's degree in English and has one published novel. This piece is especially poignant for her, and she is excited for it to be included in her first anthology.

Nikki Pennella, a New York native turned Floridian since '95, is a fitness, nutrition, and mindset coach, and a visionary entrepreneur. She channels her creativity through writing, painting, and drawing, passionately driven by her mission to illuminate life beyond trauma.

Nikki's journey, insights, and coined phrase, "Your hero lies within," are powerful tools she shares to help others thrive and heal. www.physiquesbynikki.com

Shana Smith was born in Hilo, Hawaii, and moved to Gainesville, Florida, with her parents and sister as a teenager. For the past twenty-five years, she has been known to many as the children's musical persona "Shana Banana," winning national awards from *Parent's Choice* and *iParenting* along with receiving two first-round Grammy nominations. Shana is the author of *Meditation for Moms and Dads: 108 Tips for Mindful Parents and Caregivers* and the novel *Islands of Cedars*, inspired by her love of wild Florida. She is currently working on her next historical fiction novel, based in Micanopy, Florida. www.oaktreeinthegarden.com

Soleil Tron is a new writer, quilt artist, jewelry maker, and avid competitive pool player. A lifelong lover of books, she hopes to bring her unique creativity, precision, and mental focus necessary for all these interests into her new passion, writing. Soleil lives with her husband near Birmingham, Alabama.

Stephen Aycock: Born 1959, Christian. Single father of 4 boys, Ryan, Chris, Gabrial, and Lukas. Grad from Walker High School and the University of Alabama at Walker College, Jasper. Retired, 35 years in the Army, 15 years active duty/20 years reserve. Retired, UAB with 23 years as an Assistant Nurse Manager. Currently writes a grief column for the *Walker Co. Leader* in Jasper, Alabama.

Stormy King: "My culture of origin was West Coast hippie. I am retired, and I live alone with my three cats in the far north of California. I love my life more than ever! I tell people it is a blast just to be me, LOL." www.ramdasslove.org

About the Editors

Becky Magnolia, otherwise known as "the fairy book-mother" is the author of fifteen books and helps other writers realize their dreams of becoming published authors. She is thrilled and honored to have had the opportunity to work with this talented group of authors (and one artist!) to manifest this little book. Becky aspires to continue sharing people's words, spreading the power of community, connection, and joy to anyone and everyone she meets. www.MagnoliaMystic.com

Karin Nicely has been working as a professional editor for more than twenty-five years, carefully polishing and perfecting each client's work while embracing their unique voice and style. She specializes in line editing and copy editing for independent authors in various fiction and non-fiction genres and is the owner of Seren Publishing, based in the Horse Capital of the World—Ocala, Florida. www.serenpublishing.com

renee 55

**To find out more about Becky Magnolia
and her book-publishing services,
please feel free to reach out:**

Becky@MagnoliaMystic.com
(904) 325 6758

www.MagnoliaMystic.com
Facebook: BeckyMagnoliaAuthor
Instagram: @authorbeckymagnolia
YouTube: @BeckyMagnolia1

A portion of the proceeds of this anthology will go to the National CARE Foundation.

The National CARE Foundation advocates for survivors of sexual assault, domestic violence, and other traumatic circumstances by connecting them with services and resources that can enhance their quality of life, as well as through community awareness. They also address social issues through sex-positive research and education.
https://ntlcarefoundation.org/